THE FILMS OF
DOLORES DEL RIO

THE FILMS

OF

DOLORES DEL RIO

BY

ALLEN L. WOLL

GORDON PRESS FILM SERIES

GORDON PRESS
NEW YORK
1978

GORDON PRESS—Publishers
P. O. Box 459
Bowling Green Station
New York, N.Y. 10004

Library of Congress Cataloging in Publication Data

Woll, Allen L
    The films of Dolores Del Rio.

    (Gordon Press film series)
    Filmography: p.
    Bibliography: p.
    1. Del Río Dolores, 1905-   I. Title.
PN2318.D4W6   791.43'028'0924   77-3420
ISBN 0-8490-1364-X

Printed in the United States of America

TO MYRA

TABLE OF CONTENTS

INTRODUCTION

Two Mexican women came to Hollywood during the 1920's. One, Dolores Del Rio, began a film career that spanned five decades. The other, Lupe Velez, committed suicide in 1944. Her short career left her stereotyped as the "Mexican Spitfire," a hot-blooded young lady who mangled the English language beyond recognition. As Hollywood's foremost image of the Mexican woman, Lupe was intemperate, passionate, and uncontrollable. From the moment she arrived in the film capital, she was trapped in a stereotype from which there was no escape. The titles of her films indicate the role she was expected to play: <u>Strictly Dynamite</u>, <u>Hot Pepper</u>, <u>Lady Of The Pavements</u>, and <u>Mexican Spitfire's Blessed Event</u>.

Lupe's career languished in a series of "Mexican Spitfire" films for RKO. The routine was funny once, perhaps even twice, but after eight films the audiences began to forsake poor Lupe.

Dolores Del Rio's career displays none of these vicissitudes. She worked for America's foremost directors (John Ford, Orson Welles, and King Vidor) and appeared with the most popular actors of the age. She bridged the gap between silent and sound film with ease, and, when her interest in Hollywood slackened, she returned to her native Mexico and dominated the nascent film industry. During this period she won four Arieles, Mexico's equivalent of the Oscar. She also performed in both Argentina and Spain before returning to the United States to appear

-1-

in John Ford's <u>Cheyenne</u> <u>Autumn</u> in 1964. She is currently
living in a suburb of Mexico City at this time, and she
still remains active. She is repeatedly honored by the
Mexican government for her contributions to the cinematic
art as well as for her charitable efforts.

Much of the reason for Dolores Del Rio's continuing
fame is the fact that she gave the Mexican people a
symbol to be proud of. Unlike Lupe Velez, Dolores Del
Rio rarely descended to the role of the comic Mexican in
her film performances. Indeed, she portrayed a woman who
just happened to be Mexican in most of her American films.
Her nationality rarely limited her choice of film roles
nor determined the manner in which they would be portrayed.
Almost singlehandedly Dolores Del Rio fractured the Latin
stereotypes that had dominated the American cinema since
its inception. She was bound by no rules and, as a result,
became one of the finest character actresses in American
films of the 1930's.

Dolores Del Rio's conquest of the Hollywood stereotypes was no mean feat. Specific boundaries limited the
portrayals of minority groups on the American screen.
Native Americans, Blacks, Jews, Russians, Germans, and
Latins had set patterns of filmic behavior based on racial
or ethnic background. Little freedom could be exercised
within these limits. Most actors belonging to these
minority groups are remembered for their ability to "play"
with these well-defined roles and carry them to ludicrous
extremes or sentimental excesses. Few were able to dis-
card these characterizations altogether.

Dolores Del Rio remains the prime exception. When
she reached Hollywood, the film industry had developed
rigidly defined rules for the behavior of the Latin. Del
Rio's key to success was her ability to eliminate these
stereotypes in the majority of her films. She alone among
Latin performers was able to shed the derogatory images of
the Mexican that had plagued Hollywood since the turn of
the century.

I. THE LATIN IMAGE IN SILENT FILMS

American audiences were shocked by the film image of their neighbors to the south. Although the majority of early silent films emphasized action and violence, the Mexican bandits were clearly among the most vile. They robbed, murdered, plundered, raped, cheated, gambled, lied, and displayed virtually every vice that could be shown on the screen.[1]

As a reward for the Mexican's degraded state, he received a new name. He was not known as a Mexican, or even an Indian, but was dubbed "the greaser," one of the screen's most despicable characters.[2] Hence, even the titles of such films as Tony the Greaser (1911), Broncho Billy and the Greaser (1914), and The Greaser's Revenge (1914) revealed an innate prejudice against the Mexican.[3]

The typical "greaser" was violent and prone to murder, as Broncho Billy discovered when he met his first greaser in 1914: "Broncho Billy, the mail carrier, ejects a greaser from the post office for pushing a girl out of the way. The half-breed is thoroughly angered and swears revenge. Billy then goes home and on the way he loses his mailbag. He does not miss it, so he goes to bed that night unaware of his loss. The girl he protected at the post office finds the mail bag, and when she approaches Billy's shack to return it, she sees the greaser prowling about. She hastens to a dance hall, where she tells her friends of Broncho's danger, and she leads the way back to his shack where they arrive just in time to save him from being stabbed while asleep."[4]

While the normal villain would primarily murder or
steal, the Mexican greaser often carried his occupation
to excess. More often than not, he enjoyed his subtle
extension of the limits of violence. A Mexican in The
Cowboy's Baby (1910) throws the hero's child into a river.
The greaser in A Western Child's Heroism (1912) attacks
the Americans who saved his life. In Broncho Billy's
Redemption (1910), a vile Mexican is given money to buy
medicine for a dying man. Instead he steals the money
and tosses away the prescription. The Greaser's Revenge
(1914) finds José, "the evil halfbreed," trying to kill
Fred by throwing him in a deserted mine shaft.

Despite the innate sense of violence among the
Mexicans, the greasers had one chance to redeem themselves.
Namely, they had to forsake their Mexican brethren, and
ally themselves with either the Americans, the land owners,
or the business executives when they were threatened by a
hoarde of attacking greasers. In this respect, the "good
greaser" becomes a correspondent to the "Uncle Tom" figure
that has been seen in films about Blacks. The loyalty is
to the master, the dominant race or nation, and never to
fellow Blacks or Mexicans.

Tony the Greaser (1911) reveals the nature of the
"good greaser." The humble Tony loves the landowner's
daughter, but as an American she cannot return his affections. A band of "dissolute Mexicans' arrive, and threaten
both the ranch and the lovely daughter. Tony eventually
saves the day, but he is killed in the process. His only
reward is to kiss the daughter's handkerchief as he expires
Here is the truly noble greaser! An ad for the film
explains that "from force of habit, some might call him a
"Greaser"; true, he is a Mexicano, but he is "a man of noble
instincts and chivalrous nature."

The key to the true nature of the Mexican can be found
in his relation to North Americans. If the greaser is
loyal and brave, he is "good." If he robs and pillages,
he becomes an object of scorn.

Whenever Mexicans are placed in conflict with North
Americans, the Yankee always wins due to his superior
moral quality and innate intelligence. The Mexican can
never hope to conquer, even if he possesses superior

-4-

military might, as The Aztec Treasure (1914) demonstrates:
"Miguel Pérez, the Governor of the Province, oppresses
and enslaves the peons of Mescalito so that they face
starvation. Miguel falls for Dolores, but luckily Miguel's
passion is turned momentarily by the capture of Dick Hen-
shaw, a Yankee insurrectionist, who has been leading the
insurrectors against the despot. His capture naturally
places the revolutionists in a precarious position since
they are entirely dependent upon their Yankee leader for
success." Dick easily manages to kill Miguel. He marries
Dolores, and discovers the hidden Aztec treasure on their
wedding night. He is then "made Governor of the Province
and devotes the treasure to the betterment and welfare
of the oppressed people."5

The Aztec Treasure also reveals two important char-
acteristics of Mexican-American relations in films that
have continued to this day. First, Mexicans are often
incapable of independent action. Here the revolutionaries
are "entirely dependent on their Yankee leader for success."
The Mexicans are thus unable to foment a revolution on their
own initiative, a "fact" which future events will soon
discredit.

Secondly, The Aztec Treasure and countless films of
the period reveal the superiority of Yankee love. When
given a choice between José or Fred in The Greaser's
Revenge, the young lady inevitably chooses the North
American. While a North American male can marry a high-
bred Mexican woman, any Mexican who desires a North American wife is only asking for trouble, as Tony the Greaser
discovered.

Despite the blantant stereotypes in these silent films,
there was very little criticism in the American press at
this time. A review of Mexican Mine Fraud (1914) is
revealing in this respect:

> Much of the action is supposed to have taken
> place in Mexico, a country with which the aver-
> age American is a lot more familiar with than
> was the director who made this picture. A sad
> slip, too, is the introduction of a half-dozen
> fine looking lions that might have been perfect-
> ly at home in South Africa, but fail to convince
> when introduced apparently as a group captured
> in Mexico by a band of lion tamers.6

Ironically, the critic paid no attention to the comic opera actions of the Mexicans in this film. Only the geographic anachronisms appeared unusual to him. In this fashion, the conventions governing the activities of the Mexican or the greaser were thus well established in the early silent films.

FROM THE MEXICAN REVOLUTION TO WORLD WAR I

"Pancho Villa tried hard to be a director. He told me to film the funeral of a general. Villa's enemies, the Federal forces, had executed him by lashing him to the tracks and driving a train over him. The funeral spread over three days. I didn't have enough film for half a day. So I cranked the camera without any film in it. It was all I could do. I didn't want to be shot myself."

--Charles Rosher[7]

With the start of the Mexican Revolution, films about the war-torn Republic became more violent than ever. Only this time the violence was real as a diverse variety of power contenders competed for control in Mexico City. The difference between motion pictures of revolutions and the actual events began to blur, as one of the leading agrarian revolutionaries, Pancho Villa, signed a contract with the Mutual Film Corporation. For $25,000, the rebel hero allowed Mutual cameramen to follow his exploits. In return, he agreed to fight during daylight hours if possible, and try to delay his attacks until the cameras were in position.

Villa agreed to this contract since his forces needed money for munitions. Gunther Lessing, a young lawyer, arranged the deal with Villa and deposited a healthy sum in an El Paso bank. Mutual also signed agreements for a second feature, a life of Villa, to be directed by D. W. Griffith.

Raoul Walsh was sent to Mexico to shoot background footage and action scenes for this film. Walsh was given little advice for his maiden film effort. Frank Woods suggested to Walsh that he "think up a story that the general will like and for God's sake never refer to him

-6-

as a bandit. As far as we're concerned he's a liberator."[8]

Villa approved of the young director. His lieutenant, Manuel Ortega, replied, "The general says he will be
pleased for you to make the story. And he will take good
care of you, because if you are killed there will be no
picture for the world to see."

Griffith was too busy filming The Birth Of A Nation
to complete the Villa film, so the assignment was given
to Christy Cabanne. The young Walsh was assigned the
role of the agrarian hero as a youth in The Life Of Villa.
Villa himself approved the casting.[9]

The Hollywood cameramen who arrived in Mexico
finally met the Mexicans that they had been portraying
on the screen. The real life variety of the "greaser"
did little to change Hollywood denizens' preconceived
notions. Mexico remained a violent and brutal land. A
Pathe cameraman, Fritz Wagner, related his experiences:
"When I left the City of Mexico for Torreón, I intended
to be back in two or three weeks, but since then I have
been learning that what a Mexican promises and what he
fulfills are two different things. A letter fully de-
tailing my experiences would be 30,000 words long and
such a letter is, of course, impossible."

"For a couple of days I had nothing to eat and was
forced to drink from the mud puddles of the road. The
consequence was that when I reached Saltillo, when coming
back, I was sick, deadly sick, and became little more
than skin and bones. I am not afraid, whatever may happen,
but I never thought I would come out alive from this trip."

"I have seen four big battles. On each occasion I
was threatened with arrest from the Federal general if I
took any pictures. He also threatened on one occasion
when he caught me turning the crank to smash the camera.
He would have done so, too, but for the fact that the
rebels came pretty close just then and he had to take it
on the run to save his hide."

"At Lagruna the battle became a rout and the dis-
organization of the Federal forces was complete. Napoleon's
retreat from Moscow was but a disaster on a larger scale.
It was every man for himself and the Devil (or the rebels)
take the hindmost. I had saved my film and camera (60 lbs.)

and went on foot with this load through the desert for 25 miles. I saw my end coming. Nobody would carry my stuff nor could I get a horse at any price. Finally I met a friendly Indian, who brought me to La Hipólita."

"For five nights I lay on the stones without a blanket, with my films for a pillow and my camera in my arm. I was afraid to take more than broken naps for fear my camera would be stolen. As it was when I finally got back to Mexico after breaking jail I had left only a shirt, trousers, coat and a pair of shoes. All the rest the rebels got. I tried hard to save my films, but I guess I am lucky at that. Those that I brought with me I had in my pockets. The rest made fine kindling for the campfires of the rebels."

"When I arrived in the City of Mexico I got another camera from the Pathe agent there and got busy again. When Huerta heard I was back he sent two secret service men to the hotel, who confiscated all my papers and films. They did leave the camera. From then on I had the unpleasant experience of seeing myself constantly shadowed. Any time I would open the door of my room there would be a murderous-looking individual standing near by. At the dining table would be another, who would scarce take his eyes from me. I became so nervous that the running of a mouse across the room at night would make me jump up in the bed in a cold sweat. I expected every moment to either be thrown into some dungeon or else knifed in the back. A man can stand an out and out fight -- it is the deadly danger constantly impending that wears a man out."

"Finally one day Huerta sent for me and told me to develop the films (under supervision) and project them for him. He censored the films, had me cut out all the parts unfavorable to the Federals and then ordered the 'Salon Rojo' show them as advertising for his troops. Huerta was much pleased with his show, otherwise I would have lost the films. I saw my chance and decided to beat it before another storm broke. I told the Chief of Police that Huerta had O.K.'d the films and that it was all right for me to go to Vera Cruz. The Chief was very decent and gave me his card, which I used as a passport. I hid myself in a freight car and finally got to Vera Cruz O.K."

"When Victor Miller, your cameraman, arrived with a new outfit for me, for the first time in weeks I was able to eat with an appetite and sleep as a man should sleep."10

Considerable hoopla surrounded the first showings of <u>Barbarous Mexico</u>, also known as <u>War in Mexico</u>, in 1913. The resulting films were unusually violent. The <u>New York Times</u> praised the film at its premiere, noting that "there are many scenes in which General Villa is seen directing the movement of his troops and artillery, and cavalry battles are shown with remarkable clearness. Other views show the burning of dead bodies on the battlefield."11

During the Revolutionary period, Hollywood received its first inkling that Latins might not appreciate their standard film image. This incident occurred in Monclova, Mexico, where Solax features was filming a conventional Western. Two of the Mexican extras became enraged because the story called for their capture by the American heroes. As a result, they changed the script and fired their guns at the Americans. Fortunately, the guns contained blank cartridges, but the affair started a fight between the American crew and the Mexicans. Soldiers were called in to quell the fighting, and the culprits were flogged with the flat end of the sword.12

World War I did far more to end the derogatory portrayals of the American screen than did any isolated incidents or complaints from South American governments. A variety of notions caused this abrupt change which led to the virtual elimination of the word <u>greaser</u> in films appearing after 1917. First of all, there was a shift of villains. Now, the Kaiser and the Hun were the enemy, not the Mexican next door.

Secondly, the European war made the export of French or British films to Latin America much more difficult. For the first time, Hollywood had an opportunity to make commercial inroads in a vast territory it had formerly ignored. Arthur T. Lang, export manager of the Nicholas Power Company, explained that the time was ripe for Hollywood: "But now, an entirely new situation -- as remarkable as it was unexpected -- has arisen, opening the way to the rapid development of export trade in American films and providing an opportunity not merely for the pioneers, but for all the film manufacturers of the country to cash in heavily."13

If Hollywood hoped to expand its markets during this period, derogatory views of the Latin had to be shunned. As a result, the greaser almost disappeared from the screen.

Interestingly, the Latin was not replaced, for the time being, by a new Mexican, intelligent, cultured, and refined. The only way that Hollywood could deal with its stock character was to eliminate it, and not change it.

The film industry cultivated its new market with a passion, after certain cultural misunderstandings had been alleviated. The first major problem was the language barrier. Film distributors insisted on using English in their catalogues and correspondence. F. C. Roberts, of the San Juan, Puerto Rico, Bureau of Labor, wrote a letter to Moving Picture World explaining the difficulties that might arise from this practice: "In Latin America there is not even one for every three thousand that speaks English. They only speak Spanish or Portuguese and these are the languages they use exclusively for everything. Therefore, when these people receive a catalogue printed in English, it produces the same effect as if the American people were to receive catalogues in Chinese."14

A few months after this complaint appeared, Motion Picture World established a Spanish edition, Cine-Mundial, to facilitate the film distribution process in South America. The advertisements for the new trade magazine proclaimed that it "is edited by natives of Spanish speaking countries. These men have a wide and intimate knowledge of conditions in our Latin sister-Republics. They speak the real language of these countries, not a poor imitation!"15

At virtually the same time, a new process of subtitling was developed. Rather than providing each print with Spanish language subtitles, each nation prepared its own subtitles for the American films. These were then printed and projected alongside the English titles by the use of a separate projector. Once the showings were completed, the films could then be returned unchanged to the American distributor.16

The result of this active catering to South American markets led to a marked increase in the number of American films shown. One foreign visitor to Rio in 1916 complained that "it took a considerable search to find anything but American-made films."17 Interestingly, although Hollywood showed a marked economic interest in South America, there was no attempt to woo this new audience with films about their own native land. Latins viewed the same films

-10-

American audiences saw during this time period. Such films as <u>Tillie's Tomato Surprise</u>, <u>The Riddle of the Silk Stocking</u>, <u>The Right Girl</u>, and <u>In the Shadows of the Pyramids</u> were among the most popular films in Argentina in 1916.[18] American distributors viewed this interest in North America as quite natural: "Just as our people like to see films representing conditions in far-away lands, so are Latin audiences interested in films showing American life, institutions, humor and scenery. They like our clean-cut romances and they enjoy films with a strong touch of industrialism, especially if it borders on the spectacular, and they are keen for our western pictures."[19]

During the wartime period there were few attacks on film producers for presenting Latins in an unfavorable light. This was due primarily to the disappearance of the Mexican villain on the screen and the substitution of the treacherous Hun. Indicative of the calm in the relationship between the Latin countries and the motion picture producers was the placid session at the Pan-American Conference in Buenos Aires. Normally these meetings are hectic affairs which allow the South American nations to vent their wrath at American policy. Here, only financial matters were discussed with film distributors in such sessions as "The Necessity of Better Transportation Facilities in the American Republics," "Improved Banking Facilities," and "The Copyright Situation." No one mentioned the Latin image in film, an issue that had disturbed international conferences earlier in the century.[20]

Thus, while Hollywood achieved what was primarily an economic goal, both government officials and newspapers praised the film-makers' good-will in these troubled times: "The closer union of the two Americas is one of the gratifying things that is coming out of the great war cloud whose silver lining has so long been hidden. It is hoped that the Western Hemisphere will never be subjected to the hatreds and misunderstandings that have wrought such destruction in the Eastern. Men of vision in all the countries concerned should work toward harmony both now and in the future."[21]

The wartime rhetoric seemed to portend a glowing period in inter-American relations. The greaser had apparently vanished and Hollywood might continue its enterprise of goodwill. However, with the ending of the war, the bubble burst, and disreputable Latins returned once again to the American screen.

Whither the Greaser?

> At the present time there is
> a picture in one of the lead-
> ing Broadway theatres purport-
> to have a "Brazilian" mien.
> One of the characters has the
> name Alvadorez. This is not
> a Brazilian name, and I be-
> lieve it was taken from some
> make of cigar.
>
> Letter to editor, <u>New York Times</u>[22]

The fragile facade of inter-American unity was
shattered after the war, and previous stereotypes returned
to the American screen. An advertisement for the film
<u>Rio Grande</u> made it appear as though the interregnum of
the war years had never occurred: "Take the hot blood of
Mexico and mix it fifty-fifty with the cooler, calmer
strain of the Northern neighbor and what happens? You
can gamble on it that the daughter of the union will blow
hot, blow cold,...that she will be passionate, revengeful,
brave, unreasonable, and most cussedly loveable."

Rex Beach, the novelist, explorer, and motion picture producer also turned his attention to the lands
south of the border, and claimed to discover an isle of
cannibals, "A savage people who know scarcely anything
of the great world revolving around them, and, astonish-
ingly, still cling to the practice of eating their own
kind." He dismissed Mexico as "an unkempt land, rather
careless of its civilization," and noted that "it is not
an unusual thing to travel with an armored car both fore
and aft."[23]

By this time, Mexico had had enough. It was no
longer going to be ridiculed on the screens of the world.
In late 1919, the Mexican government sent a formal letter
to film producers, protesting their emphasis on "films of
squalor." The pronouncement explained that "these films
do not portray the average conditions in the country."
Rather, the government contended that "photographers
travel about, seeking the worst conditions they can find,
and compose their films entirely of such pictures." The
letter ended with a subtle warning, as the government
threatened to restrict motion picture photography in
Mexico.

This informal warning did little to change Hollywood practices, as <u>Rio Grande</u> and the Rex Beach episode reveal. By February, 1922, the Mexican government decided to ban all films that portrayed Mexicans unfavorably. By itself, this action would have done little to restrict Hollywood productions which cast Mexicans as villains. The offending film could still be distributed to other countries and little profit would be lost. As a result, the Mexican government decided to ban <u>all films</u> produced by the company which produced the offensive film. This was quite a strong ultimatum to be delivered at the height of the American film industry's expansion southward. The Famous Players-Lasky offices, which had just completed a one hundred film deal with Mexican distributors, was shaken by the pronouncement and issued a statement saying that "the wishes of the government would be respected."

The reasons for this action was obvious. A high official of the Mexican government explained that "the usual portrayal of the Mexican in moving pictures is as a bandit or a sneak. Ill will toward Mexico has been inflamed by these pictures to such an extent, that the Mexican government found it necessary to make such a protest."[24]

Mexico was not alone in its ban of film companies that offended national sentiments. Panama followed soon after with similar legislation, after the filming of <u>Ne'er-Do-Well</u> (1923) on its soil. Bad vibrations began soon after the cast and crew arrived. Lila Lee, the female star, was quoted as saying that she "had lived largely on iguanas while in Panama," a remark quite far from the truth. She was forced to apologize publicly so the film company would not be expelled. The film itself also offended Panamanian audiences, since once again Latin society was portrayed as primitive and the Latin Lover loses the woman to a North American.

<u>The</u> <u>Ne'er-Do-Well</u> is Kirk Anthony (Thomas Meighan), the idle son of a millionaire. He has only two interests-- women and wine. One night, after sipping a little too much of the spirits, Kirk's rich friends deposit him on a freighter bound for Panama. He arrives at the Canal without a cent. His only possession is a white shirt with the phone numbers of his girlfriends written on the back. He immediately falls in love with Chiquita (Lila Lee),

the daughter of a Panamanian politician. Kirk easily
steals Chiquita from her current beau, Ramón Alfarez
(Sid Smith), a diminuitive police inspector. Ramon
hasn't a chance once Chiquita spots the North American.
He becomes jealous, but it is to no avail. Kirk marries
Chiquita and returns to his father's estate. Once again,
the so-called Latin Lover is found lacking.[25]

The Panamanian legislation surpassed that of the
Mexican in severity. Article seven of the legislation
proclaimed that "the filming and exhibition of films
tending to discredit or lower the prestige of the country,
or which may in any form involve propaganda prejudicial
to the moral, social, and economic interests of the
nation are prohibited." Films were not alone in this vast
censorship based on questions of prestige. Reporters might
be expelled for "transmitting prejudicial news." Even
the makers of postal cards had to beware. Anyone who
produced photographs which "discredit the race or mis-
represent national customs" would be fined heavily.[26]

What was Hollywood to do? How could it replace its
most popular and most thoroughly vile villain. A French,
Dutch, or Italian substitution would merely offend European audiences. The solution lie in the abandoning of Mexican and Central American locales and switching scenes
to the Argentine, some several thousand miles away. The
result of the Mexican restrictions was merely to move the
standard Latin-American stereotypes to a new location.
Thus, the domination of Mexican locales in Hollywood
films vanished in the 1920's as producers sought to avoid
the troublesome restrictions. The Latin's new homes were
now Brazil and Argentina, areas that had been rarely considered in the first two decades of the century.

One of the first films of this scenic shift, Argentine
Love (1924), featured Ricardo Cortez and Bebe Daniels, in
a standard Latin style love story. Bebe Daniels, portraying an Argentine, falls in love with a North American
stranger. This angers Ricardo, a "hot-blooded Argentinian,"
and he vows to murder anyone who looks at Bebe. Bebe
pretends to love Ricardo so he will not harm her true love.
As Ricardo is about to attack Bebe, he is suddenly shot.
All ends happily, and the lovers are reunited. The film
was reputedly so trite and poorly acted that a critic for
the New York Times commented: "In the end the American and
heroine are so glad that it is all over that they give a
blase glance at the bullet ridden body of the hot-headed
man." He could imagine the director saying at the finale,

"Get ready with the tears when I clap my hands. Look
as Spanish as you can -- except the hero!"[27]

The Gaucho arrived on the screens shortly thereafter, and it offered little improvement in the stock
portrayal of Latin Americans, whether Mexican or Argentine.
At first it seemed that his film might display technical
accuracy. Doublas Fairbanks, the star of the film, insisted on learning to use the bola, the weapon of the
gauchos, with consummate proficiency. Fairbanks insisted
that Argentine experts, Nick Milanesio and Andrés
Rodríguez, be flown to Hollywood for several months.
Fairbanks later claimed that it took him longer to use the
bolas than to make the film. Not only did Fairbanks have
to learn to use the bola, but his two hundred cohorts in
the film had to master the weapon. Ironically, Fairbank's
sidekicks were mostly Mexican.   Therefore, as one expert
explained, "the bola was as unfamiliar to them as croquet
to an American Indian or baseball to an Eskimo."[28]   Interestingly, the Mexicans were once again bandits, even
though the film proclaimed them Argentine gauchos.

Once the crew of two hundred and one "gauchos"
learned to use the bolas, all attempts at technical accuracy were stopped. The story itself bore no relation to
the Argentine, or anywhere else in South America. Fairbanks admitted that he conceived the idea for the story
while visiting Our Lady of Lourdes in France! The Gaucho
concerns a victim of the "black doom" (leprosy). Fairbanks antagonizes a leper at a fiesta when he proclaims
that "anyone suffering from the disease ought to go forth
and put an end to himself." The gaucho's sentiments are
put to the test when he, too, contracts the disease after
a struggle with Lupe Velez, who is a Mexican portraying
an Argentine. The Madonna appears and tells the gaucho
to visit her holy shrine. Fairbanks follows her bidding
and is eventually cured of leprosy.

Where the Argentine solution appeared impractical to
producers desirous of using stock Latin villains, another
alternative arose. Rather than using the name of a real
country, and possible offending its inhabitants, screenwriters began to create mythical cities and nations.
The Dove (1928), directed by Roland West, provides the
most notorious example. The film concerns Don José María
y Sandoval (Noah Berry), who considers himself "the bes'
dam caballero in Costa Roja." Costa Roja, as the title

cards explain, is located in the Mediterranean!

This unsubtle guise hardly fooled anyone. Mordaunt
Hall, critic for the New York Times, explained: "Taken
by and large, José is perhaps a screen character to which
the Mexican government might have objected, for he is
greedy, sensuous, boastful, cold blooded, irritable, and
quite a wine-bibber, but he does dress well...He hates
to have his luncheon spoiled by a noisy victim of his
shooting squad. He adores beauty, but he is inconstant."29
Thus, the Costa Roja subterfuge diffuses any possible
criticism since José is not a resident of any present day
Latin American country. Unfortunately, when The Dove was
remade during the sound era as Girl of the Rio (1932), the
screenwriters apparently forgot this distinction and
situated this film in a Mexican bordertown. As a result,
all hell broke loose, as Mexico renewed its long-standing
threat to ban motion picture companies which produced films
offensive to Mexicans.

Thus, little had changed in the first three decades
of films concerning Latin America. The Mexican remained
the same unruly bandit whether on his native soil or in
Brazil or Argentina. Hollywood remained smug in its in-
difference. As the era of the sound film dawned, South
Americans and Hollywood producers remained as far apart
as ever. A confrontation at a dinner for motion picture
advertisers in 1927 in New York City revealed the depth
of these differences. Herbert Hoover, then Secretary of
Commerce, and James J. Walker, Mayor of New York City,
attended the affair. The guests of honor were the ambas-
sadors of the Central and South American nations.

Hoover came to the podium and wlecomed his distinguished
guests. He praised the motion picture industry to the
skies: "I trust in the good faith of this great body of
men who dominate the industry in the United States to
carry out this profound obligation -- that is, that every
picture of South American life shown to our people and
every picture of North American life shown to the South
American people should carry those ideals which build for
that respect and confidence which is the real guarantee of
peace and progress." He added that the industry must
censor itself, for at no time would he sanction government
intervention in the choice of film topics or their treatment.

The South Americans in the audience were not fooled

by Hoover's words. The Chilean ambassador, Miguel
Cruchaga Montt, responded for the group, expressing the
opinions of Latin Americans on the matter. Cruchaga's
reply indicated that he was familiar with virtually
every Latin stereotype yet seen on the American screen:
"The myth of Spanish-American lovers serenading their
fair ladies under iron-grilled balconies bathed by
romantic moonlight and alive with the beauty of red
carnations; and the injustice of portraying all those
who hail from south of the Rio Grande as born villains to
be conquered by the mighty, iron-fisted, two-gunned
vigilante; and the perpetuation of such absurdities as
picturing an Argentine gentleman on his wedding day in
the brilliant dress of a bullfighter, when the colorful
Spanish entertainment is forbidden in that progressive
country--these are things that we call, with a friendly
smile of forebearance, Hollywoodisms." 30

　　　Shortly thereafter, the stereotypes of the silent
era would appear ridiculously simple. With the advent of
sound, new and more complex versions of Latin life and society could be presented on the screen. Unfortunately,
there was little improvement. As Lupe Velez later commented, "eet stinks!"

II. DOLORES DEL RIO--THE EARLY YEARS

Dolores Del Rio's early life reads like a Cinderella story. No one would have imagined that a young Mexican girl of aristocratic background would become the toast of Hollywood during the silent era. The improbability was twofold. On one hand, the Mexican elite considered the acting profession as akin to prostitution. No self-respecting Mexican would appear on the stage or in the new motion pictures. On the other hand, Hollywood had never been receptive to Mexican-American performers. Those who had appeared in North American films had been relegated to secondary and invariably stereotyped roles. Despite these obstacles, Dolores Del Rio conquered family pressure and film industry prejudice to become the most illustrious Mexican-American actress on the American screen.

Once Dolores Del Rio arrived in Hollywood, she found that her exotic background fascinated the fan magazines. Interviewers concocted lurid and exotic tales of the "Mexican Flower." Del Rio read all of these articles and found them interesting, but generally untrue: "I've liked them all--all but one. That one, melodramatic, blood-curdling in its fantastic detail, I shall never forget!"

"It related that I had fled from Pancho Villa; that
he had pursued me and I had to swim in the nude through
icy waters to escape his clutches! Surrounded by his men,
leering, threatening, in some miraculous way I eluded them,
and worked a miracle of salvation for the terrified com-
munity!"

"The incoherence of my synopsis is no more coherent
than the story. What a shame to disappoint as imaginative
a writer, but I really must deny his "Life Story Of Dolores
Del Rio." When Pancho Villa was leading those troops he
described, I was four years old. Obviously his men would
not have been tracking me down in the swamps of my country!
I am sorry, but it just wasn't, just could not have been,
true."[1]

Actually, the young Lolita Dolores Asunsolo de Martínez,
did experience the turmoil of the Mexican Revolution, but
not to the extent that this fantastic tale implies. Dolores' father, Jesús L. Asúnsolo, a prominent banker in
Durango, thought it would be prudent to leave his home
town before it was swept by the revolutionary fervor. He
put his wife, Antonia López Negrete de Asúnsolo, and his
five year old daughter on a train to Mexico City in the
winter of 1910. The women lived with relatives in the
capital until they were joined by Jesús in 1912. After
her father returned, life became more stable for Dolores.
She was enrolled in the convent of Saint Joseph, where
French was the language of instruction.[2]

Dolores Del Rio revealed mixed emotions about her
educational experience: "I was no better, no worse than
the other girls. A bit more adventurous perhaps. And
they let me do one thing I really loved. They let me
dance."

"The only punishment I ever received was for hiding
a mirror and curling my hair. Mirrors were forbidden. I
liked to look at myself. So I hid one, and was caught.
The sisters warned me."

I curled my hair and the great humiliation came when
I was marched before all the girls in the patio of the
convent and my curled head was soundly and thoroughly
ducked into the water of the lily pond. It did me no good.
I have always felt so sorry for the sisters who wanted to
change me. I still love a mirror and I still curl my hair.
So I am stubborn, you see."[3]

Dolores' stubborness continued to shock and dismay
her family. At age fifteen she decided to marry Jaime
Martinez Del Rio. He seemed a fine choice to some. This
wealthy lawyer who had been educated in Europe beguiled
the young Dolores. Yet, one factor disturbed her. An
age gap of eighteen years separated Jaime and Dolores.
As a result Jaime occasionally treated Dolores more like
a child than a wife. They immediately embarked on a two
year honeymoon to Madrid, Paris, London, and Rome.

Despite the fact that Jaime and Dolores met the
elite of European society, Dolores became "weary of the
monotony of purely social days." The newlyweds then
returned to Mexico in 1924 to begin their married life.
Soon after her arrival in Mexico, Dolores decided to
enter the University. Once again, Dolores surprised her
family by her shocking behavior: "I had enrolled to
study the history of art, but what I was studying didn't
matter. The thing that did was, "A lady did not go to
the University." Very well, I was enjoying myself huge-
ly, my status bothering me not at all."[4]

During this period, Dolores also studied music and
ballet. One morning her mother confided to her that she
was "secretly pleased that a young married woman should
study," although everyone else thought it was shocking.

These decisions of an independent young woman appeared minor pecadillos when Dolores announced to her family
that she was going to Hollywood to become an actress.
Then "I was mad! I was any of 10,000 things! To an
infinite degree, I was completely wrong!"[5]

Dolores' entry into the motion picture business
came about almost by accident. Edwin Carewe, a Hollywood
director, visited Mexico City while on his honeymoon.
He became bored by the usual tourist attractions, and
asked to see a Mexican home. A friend called Dolores
and suggested that she invite the Americans to her
house for tea. Dolores promptly agreed, and the afternoon tea party changed the direction of her life.

Dolores recalled the events of that day in vivid
detail after she became a Hollywood star: "I called
up some of my friends and said, 'I'm having a party,
picture people, come and see - help me entertain them!
And of course they were crazy about it."

"And the picture people were Mr. Carewe and Mr.
Lytell and Miss Windsor. They came at five and they
stayed till twelve! And they talked and talked and
tangoed and tangoed, and Mr. Carewe told me I ought
to be in pictures -- and I laughed. I said, 'I have
a little round nose, and I have never acted in my life!
And he say, 'But you can feel. I know you can feel,
and if you can feel, you can act!"

" 'Oh, yes, I can feel,' I say, 'I am Latin.'
Then he moves me this way and that way and around again,
and says I have the right features, that my nose, it
does not bend - then we all laugh and tango some more and
everybody have a very good time."

"The next day Mr. Carewe ask us all to go out with
him and he offers me a wonderful contract, and then I
begin to get excited, and I get very excited! And my
husband, he thought it might be lots of fun. He is
very what you call Bohemian - he like the stage and music
and artistic people."

"He said, 'Only one thing - about this Hollywood.
I do not like what they say about Hollywood. I do not
think we would like to stay in a place like Hollywood.' "

"Then I coax him a little. I tell him, 'Go see
Hollywood. You go find out about it! So he came up and
he stayed three weeks and meet everybody and he wire me -
'Hollywood fine place. Coming to get you.' "[6]

Although Jaime eventually supported Dolores' decision
to go to Hollywood, the two families thought it a disgrace
for a young Mexican woman to become an actress. She
replied, "Very well, I will be the first."[7] She then
said to herself, "Go to Hollywood to succeed. Success
brings forgiveness." Dolores delayed no longer. She
quickly packed her belongings and boarded a train for
Hollywood. Within a few years her parents would forgive
her.

III. DOLORES DEL RIO: THE SILENT YEARS

Dolores Del Rio arrived in Hollywood on August 27, 1925
in the company of her husband Jaime. As soon as she embarked from the train, studio publicity men shortened her
name. Dolores Asúnsolo y López Negrete de Martínez del
Rio was now Dolores Del Rio, Hollywood starlet. Edwin
Carewe was determined to make his discovery a star as
quickly as possible. Within a week, Dolores Del Rio
began her first film role.[1]

Carewe produced and directed Dolores Del Rio's first
film, _Joanna,_ in September 1925. She appeared in the
secondary but important role of Carlotta de Silva, the
first of many Latin temptress roles that she would portray on the American screen. _Joanna_, based on a novel
by Henry Leyford Gates (_Joanna, of the Skirts Too Short
and the Lips Too Red and the Tongue Too Pert_), presented
the dilemma of a working class woman who inherits one
million dollars.

Joanna Manners (Dorothy Mackaill), a salesgirl in a
fashion shop, mysteriously receives a massive inheritence.
Her newfound wealth attracts the attention of Frank Brandon (Paul Nicholson), playboy nephew of a bank president,
and causes a rupture in her romance with John Wilmore
(Jack Mulhall), an architect. Brandon and Anthony Eggleson (George Fawcett), Joanna's financial adviser, intro-
duce the young heiress to the worldly-wise Carlotta de
Silva (Del Rio). Carlotta teaches Joanna the life of the
rich, and as a result, Joanna almost loses her virtue.

She accidentally discovers that Eggleson and James Greyson (Edwards Davis) have bet one million dollars on her chastity. Joanna condemns the ways of the wealthy, and returns to her beloved John, her fiance in the days before riches turned her head.[2]

Carewe continued as Dolores Del Rio's mentor in her second film High Steppers, which he produced and directed in 1926. Yet another society melodrama, this film was based on Philip Hamilton Gibbs' novel Heirs Apparent: a Novel. Dolores Del Rio again appeared in a secondary role as Evelyn Iffield, the girlfriend of hero Julian Perryam (Lloyd Hughes).

The dissolute young Julian is expelled from Oxford for his high-living ways. He returns to the family mansion, but his parents are too busy to be interested in his concerns. Adding to the young man's despair is Evelyn Iffield's refusal to marry him. He returns to London and meets Audrey Nye (Mary Astor), who had also been expelled from school. She finds him a job as a reporter on the staff of The Truth. Julian discovers that the corrupt publisher Victor Buckland (Edwards Davis) is stealing from a charity fund. An irate mob kills the thieving Buckland, and all is set right. Julian then marries his true love, Audrey, who aided him in the Buckland investigation.

Pals First, another Carewe production, promoted Dolores Del Rio to the feminine lead in this comedy of mistaken identity. Francis Perry Elliott's novel, Pals First: a Romance of Love and Comradery (1915), provided the source for this 1926 film.

Harry Chilton (Edward Earle), a young doctor, suggests that his cousin needs a lengthy rest. Richard Castleman (Lloyd Hughes) agrees with this advice and leaves on a several month sea voyage. As soon as Castleman leaves, Chilton takes advantage of his absence, and begins courting Castleman's girlfriend Jeanne Lamont (Dolores Del Rio). News arrives that Richard has been killed in a shipwreck, and Chilton, overjoyed by the news, steps up his efforts to marry Jeanne and take over the family fortune.

Meanwhile, two crooks, Dominie (Alex Francis) and the Squirrel (George Cooper), find a wounded seaman named Danny Rowland at the sea's edge. They take the ailing sailor to the nearest mansion which is owned by Castleman.

Since Rowland resembles the late Mr. Castleman, he is
greeted by all as if he has returned from the dead. As
this masquerade continues, the two crooks pretend that
Dominie is an English cleric and the Squirrel, an Italian
count. Jeanne apparently is fooled by the trio, as she
believes that her lover has returned. Chilton, however,
in danger of losing a fortune, discovers the true identity
of the men. But Danny Rowland has another surprise for
the greedy Chilton. He reveals that he actually <u>is</u>
Richard Castleman. He pretended that he was dead in order
to return in disguise and expose the illicit plans of his
cousin. He also explains that his trickery has had
another beneficial result as both Dominie and the Squirrel
resolve to reform. Chilton is disgraced, and Jeanne and
Richard are reunited.

A 1925 Anita Loos play provided the inspiration for
Dolores Del Rio's first comedy, <u>The Whole Town's Talking</u>,
released in 1926. The young hero, portrayed by Edward
Everett Horton, provides most of the film's comic touches.

Chester Binney (Horton), rendered unconscious during a
World War I battle, believes that a metal plate was
placed in his head and that he must avoid all excitement.
Actually, he has heard the diagnosis for another man, and
he thinks it is his own. Chester returns to his home-
town in his continuing search for peace and quiet.
Chester's former boss, George Simmons (Otis Harlan) discovers that the young man is about to inherit a fortune.
As a result, he tries to interest Chester in the charms
of his daughter Ethel (Virginia Lee Corbin).

Ethel is bored by the mild-mannered Chester and she
repeatedly resists his advances. Her father, however,
with greenbacks in his eyes, is not to be deterred. He
concocts a phony romance with Rita Renault (Dolores Del
Rio), a famous movie star, in order to prove to his daughter that Chester has sex appeal. George casually leaves
an autographed picture from the actress in the parlor,
so all may know of Chester's supposed affair.

By pure coincidence, Rita and her jealous husband
Jack Shields (Malcolm Waite) arrive in town for a publicity
tour. Jack spots the photo and later sees his wife kissing
Chester on the cheek for a publicity photograph. He is
enraged and begins a fight with Chester. At this time
Chester discovers that he does not have a metal plate in

his head so he begins to fight in earnest. He not only knocks out Jack, but he also flattens Donald Mont-Allen (Robert Ober), Ethel's other beau. Ethel is so impressed by Chester's display of manly courage, that she finally agrees to marry him.

Dolores Del Rio's first four films are hardly remembered at present day. Yet, her fifth film, What Price Glory?. is considered one of the classics of the silent film era. The New York Times chose it as one of the year's ten best films and its reviewer praised it as a "powerful screen effort." The article continued: "War is stripped of its glamour and there are moments when Kipling's lines "Where there ain't no ten commandments and a man can raise a thirst" fit this subject. How Quirt out-wits Flagg is so successfully accomplished by Raoul Walsh, the director, that not only was there many an explosion of laughter, but the audiences reached such a high pitch of enthusiasm that they applauded loudly."[3] The film was a financial as well as a critical success. It grossed $780,000 in four weeks at the Roxy Theater in New York. Demand for tickets was so intense that the film was shown twenty-four hours a day during the last two weeks of its run.[4]

The Fox Film Corporation paid $100,000 for the rights to the Maxwell Anderson and Laurence Stallings stage play. The theater version had shocked and impressed drama audiences with its anti-war attitudes and its realistic presentation of the language of soldiers. Burns Mantle's opening night review explained this sense of surprise: "One of the famous first nights in the theater-going history of New York is that on which What Price Glory? was introduced to a slightly startled audience. For the first time a play was presented with something resembling liberal realism, and spoken with more regard for a reasonable verisimilitude than for the sensibilities of convention-protected auditors. The shock was severe, particularly to the ladies."[5]

The problem of the play's language bothered director Raoul Walsh, who realized that he could not depend on dialogue in this silent film. He later recalled: "For the first time, I found myself hating the idea of evolving a shooting script for a picture to which the titles would be added after I was done. This would leave the protag-onists at the mercy of some censor-cowed caption editor who might or might not have understood the author's

-26

intention...I could not hope to startle the viewers with the stage dialogue. Instead the action would have to put the message across. I wondered if I could do it."[6]

Walsh's fears were relieved as Fox agreed with his choices for the lead roles. Walsh passed over the stage performers Louis Wolheim and William Boyd for starring roles. Instead he chose Victor McLaglen for the part of Captain Flagg and Edmund Lowe for the role of his arch-rival Sergeant Quirt. All that remained was the part of Charmaine, lover to both Flagg and Quirt. After a long search, Walsh recalls he "found her in one of the loveli-est girls to come out of Mexico. Her name was Dolores Del Rio."

As the film begins, the friendly rivalry between Quirt and Flagg is immediately established. Quirt and Flagg are professional soldiers serving as guards in Peking, China. A title card explains that they love to "fight, make love, and drink." Shanghai Mabel (Phyllis Haver) walks by and bends over. Both men are attracted by her charms. She invites both gentlemen to her boudoir, and when each discovers the other's presence they fight and wreck Mabel's apartment. Mabel shouts for the police. The marines arrive and take both soldiers to jail.

Quirt and Flagg's fatal attraction for the same girl gets them into trouble once again in the Philippines. Flagg leaves his beloved Carmen (Elena Jurado) in the carriage while he enters a nearby bar to purchase some wine. Quirt spots the carriage and takes to the hills with Carmen. He waves a cheerful good-bye to **an** angered Flagg.

The scene changes to France in 1914, "a land laid waste." The marines arrive in 1917 to help the French citizens. Leading the American forces is Flagg, now a captain. Flagg enters Cognac Pete's Inn and spots a familiar derriere. It is Charmaine ("Thrilled by the war in her front yard--Fascinated by the men who come to view her as they go to die."). Charmaine shows Flagg that she is a strong woman. He then asks for a room upstairs so he may be close to Charmaine.

The irascible Cognac Pete arrives, sees the soldiers, and tells his daughter Charmaine to "give them nothing free." The independent Charmaine replies, "Go jump in zee canal." Even in the title cards, Dolores Del Rio has an accent.

-27-

Flagg returns and discovers that the enlisted men are
flirting with Charmaine. He chases them from the Inn.
He then gives Charmaine a small present - a box of
Official U.S. Marine garters. As she puts them on,
Flagg turns away. He is too shy to look at his beloved.

As Flagg begins to dance with Charmaine, a messenger
arrives. Flagg and his men must go to the front.
Charmaine is upset by the news, but she bravely waves as
the soldiers leave.

Flagg returns shortly with only eighty of his men
remaining alive after the battle. The stench of death
haunts him. Charmaine embraces her "Capitaine", and
they resolve to enjoy his ten day leave.

Young men arrive in town to replace the dead. The
title card dubs them "cannon fodder." Flagg interviews
the new recruits. One is a painter, the second a farmer,
and yet another has joined the army to escape from his
mother-in-law. One boy is crying. He has lost his
identification tag. If he is killed in battle his
mother will not know he has been killed. Flagg give him
his own tag as a substitute. Flagg laments, "There is
something wrong with a world that has to wet its soil
with the blood of these boys every thirty years." By
this time the audience realizes that this film is not
going to be the rollicking soldier comedy as the first
scenes suggest. From these scenes forward the horrors
of war increase in intensity.

Flagg is summoned to the town of Bar-le-duc. Charmaine
wishes to join him, but Flagg forbids it: "There are
generals there who eat little country girls. Charmaine
is irate: "You no love me. I no wear your geeft."
As she is speaking, Sergeant Quirt appears. Flagg tries
to hide Charmaine from Quirt, but it is too late. The
damage is done. Charmaine finds Quirt attractive, so
Flagg locks her in her room. Flagg has mixed feelings
about Quirt's arrival. On one hand, he is a "jinx", yet,
he is also an experienced soldier. Flagg decides he
needs the sergeant's skills, so they bury the hatchet.
Nevertheless, their language is so strong, that Charmaine
must cover her ears as she attempts to listen from the
next room.

Flagg leaves for Bar-le-duc, and Quirt is left alone
with Charmaine. Quirt shows her magic tricks and she is

enchanted with him. He gives her his sharpshooting
medal as a token of his affection. While Quirt is courting Charmaine, Flagg is busy drinking, dancing, and
kissing in Bar-le-duc. "This is the best war I ever
attended," he tells the bar girls. When his "business"
ends, Flagg returns home by motorcycle. He is so drunk,
the cycle overturns and he must be carried to Cognac
Pete's. As he returns he calls for Charmaine. At the same
moment, Pete enters and shouts, "Someone has slept with
my daughter!"

The following title cards speed by in French rather
than English, in order to censor the proceedings. Pete
wants the offender to marry his daughter and give him
five hundred francs in damages. Flagg is worried that
he will be assumed the guilty party, but then Quirt
walks by. On his sleeve is Flagg's garter belt. Flagg
is relieved, and he laughs with joy. As the shotgun
marriage is about to occur, the troops are once again
called to the front. This would seem to save Quirt,
but Flagg insists they marry before Quirt marches off to
battle. Flagg even brings the Mayor to perform the ceremony. Yet, at the last moment, Charmaine refuses to
marry Quirt. Angered by her father's scheming, she shouts,
"My heart--she ees my own. I don't sell eet." Quirt
has the last laugh, and he thumbs his nose at Flagg. They
both march off to battle promising Charmaine they will
return.

As the horrors of war continue, a title card reads,
"Captain Flagg--Stop the blood." The latest casualty is
Mother's boy, the young man without an identification tag.
Flagg cries as the youth expires in his arms. Flagg is
tired "of white faced boys with the stink of death in
their nostrils." Another soldier attempts to flee, and
Lieutenant Moore (Leslie Fenton) speaks to him of honor
and courage. The frightened recruit asks as men are
dying, "What price glory, now?"

Then, "when the blood and youth of nations had been
sacrificed for the capture of a village," the battle ends.
Most of Flagg's soldiers survive and they remain in the
battle zone. Quirt's leg has been injured, so he returns
to Charmaine's village. Flagg jokingly claims that Quirt
wounded himself on purpose so he can see his lover once
again.

Charmaine is pleased her men have returned, but she
cries when she hears "Mother's boy" has been killed.
She goes to the local cemetery ("The Field Of Glory"), and
buries unopened letters from his Mother at the youth's
graveside. She then cleans the gravestone and returns
to the Inn.

On her return she discovers Quirt has arrived. They
embrace, and she helps the wounded soldier sit by her
side. She begins to make him dinner as Flagg returns.
Flagg asserts that the issue must be decided. Who will
marry Charmaine? They decide to draw cards for her.
Flagg switches cards at the last moment and Quirt loses
the draw. Flagg wins, but Charmaine shouts, "Quirt has
all my love." Flagg realizes Quirt has won and he nobly
retires.

As Flagg climbs the stairs a messenger arrives once
again. Flagg must return to the front. He vacillates,
and ponders telling the messenger to say that he was
unable to find him. Yet, he hears the trumpet call, and
he must return to battle: "This war racket sounds sort of
like a religion--the bugle calls, we answer." Charmaine
is proud of Flagg: "I salute you Flagg. You are a brave
man."

Quirt returns and he embraces Charmaine. Yet, he too
hears the trumpet. As he stands at attention, he decides
that he must also join the battle. He shouts, "Hey Flagg,
wait for Baby." Charmaine watches him leave and laments,
"They came back once; they came back twice; they will
not come back three times." Quirt and Flagg embrace and
march to war as Charmaine shouts in agony. "They are too
young to die."

Not only did What Price Glory? earn critical raves for
the young actress, but it also allowed Dolores Del Rio to
portray a woman like herself. She claimed that she
identified with Charmaine: "I am not, by nature, melan-
choly, weepy, sorrowful, languishing or sweet. I am not
patient. I am not conventional. I am not Ramona nor am
I an Evangeline. More, I am the girl of What Price Glory?
There, for a bit, I could show my real self. I am, by
nature, tempestuous, fiery, stormy, eager."[7]

Dolores Del Rio followed What Price Glory? with another
Edwin Carewe production based on Tolstoy's novel Resurrection. Del Rio portrays Katusha, an orphaned peasant girl in

St. Petersburg. Prince Dimitri (Rod La Rocque) notices
the young peasant woman and seduces her. After their
brief affair, Dimitri returns to his regiment leaving
Katusha alone. Katusha's aunt discovers the young girl
is pregnant and chases her from her home. Weakened by
months of hunger, Katusha gives birth to a dead child.
She becomes a prostitute and is falsely imprisoned on
the charge of murdering and robbing a merchant. Dimitri
returns and is placed on the jury at her trial. Dimitri
feels pangs of conscience and offers to marry Katusha.
She loves the Prince, but she decides to carry the burden
alone. Although innocent, she is exiled to Siberia.
She leaves Dimitri and serves her lengthy sentence alone.

Raoul Walsh, the director of What Price Glory?,
returned to direct Dolores Del Rio in her next film The
Loves Of Carmen in 1927. Based on the Prosper Mérimée
story and the Bizet opera, this new version of Carmen was
presented in a tinted lavender print. Moving Picture
World described the plot as follows: "Carmen (Del Rio),
a gypsy, working in a Spanish cigar factory, is flaunted
by Escamillo (Victor McLaglen), the bullfighter, but
infatuates José (Don Alvarado), a soldier, who aids her
to escape from jail and follows her to the gypsy camp.
Tiring of his love, Carmen finally fascinates Escamillo
and the love-crazed José kills her at a bull fight just
as Escamillo is being proclaimed by the audience."[8]

Walsh enjoyed directing The Loves Of Carmen and had only
words of praise for his female star:"An outstanding
memory...is that Dolores Del Rio treated her lovers like
a black widow spider. By now the beautiful Mexican was
a star in her own right. The way in which she portrayed
a female Casanova left me with little to worry about
while she was on camera. She ran through her admirers
like Rahab of Jericho. Their fawning antics gave me an
idea. I sent for a dozen red roses. She smiled when I
handed her the longest one and prompted her in what to do.
When the suitor who obviously considered her the front-
runner knelt humbly at her feet, she used the rose as a
gentle whip to make him grovel. The viewers loved it
and we got a kind press review."[9]

In 1928 Dolores Del Rio appeared in The Gateway Of The
Moon, a South American melodrama. George Gillespie
(Anders Randolf) must complete a Bolivian railway within
the year. In order to accomplish this task, he ruthlessly
exploits the native workers. The railway firm sends
Arthur Wyall (Walter Pidgeon) to inspect the job. Wyatt

discovers Gillespie's cruelty and vows to report him to
the company. Gillespie decides the only way to solve
his problem is to have Wyall killed. Toni (Del Rio) a
halfbreed, discovers Gillespie's plan and saves him from
death.

Del Rio followed this film with Ramona, based on the
Helen Hunt Jackson novel of the persecution of the
American Indian in early California. Edwin Carewe, of
Chickasaw Indian descent, professed a fondness for the
novel as soon as he read it. He directed it, and his
brother Finis Fox wrote the screenplay. Once again,
Dolores Del Rio portrays a halfbreed.[10]

Señora Morena (Vera Lewis) adopts the young Ramona
(Del Rio). She is a cruel woman who only shows kindness
to her son Felipe (Roland Drew). Ramona discovers her
true ancestry and elopes with Allessandro (Warner Baxter),
an Indian brave. Life in the mountains is difficult for
Ramona and Allesandro. Their daughter is killed by a
bandit, and Alessandro is killed by a rancher. Ramona
becomes an amnesiac and wanders aimlessly through the
California hills. Felipe discovers her and attempts to
restore her memory. All is futile until he sings a song
from their childhood days. The melody jogs Ramona's
memory and she remembers everything.

The ballad which returns Ramona's memory is the aptly
titled "Ramona" by Mabel Wayne and L. Wolfe Gilbert.
Dolores Del Rio actually performed the song at several
theaters which were playing the film. More importantly,
"Ramona" became Del Rio's one and only recording. RCA
Victor has resurrected the 1928 disc on a recent album
entitled Stars Of The Silver Screen (LPV-538). The
record is revealing in several respects. Del Rio had an
extremely capable, if not good singing voice. She sings
effortlessly, and seems to have no trouble reaching several
high notes. Yet, this recording betrays the fact that
Del Rio still had a heavy accent. Most of the lyrics are
unintelligible, and those that can be deciphered reveal
a lingering Spanish dialect. Fortunately, the silent
films cloaked this infirmity. Yet, by this date,
dialogue had already begun to appear in motion pictures.
As Del Rio later revealed, she worried constantly about
her accent. Perhaps, for this reason, she delayed her
first sound film until 1930. By that date, her accent
had almost disappeared.

While _Ramona_ ended happily, Del Rio's personal life
was becoming plagued with problems. As she completed
Ramona, her marriage to Jaime Martínez Del Rio collapsed.
She filed suit for divorce in Nogales, Mexico, in June,
1928, after a four month trial separation from Jaime.
He claimed at that time that he was tired of being known
as "Dolores Del Rio's husband", so he left Hollywood for
New York to pursue a career as a writer.[11]

Jaime's independence was brief. Blood poisoning following an operation on a boil left him in a delirious fever
while on vacation in Berlin. He died in December after
a two week illness. Dolores was unable to see her former
husband before his death, but she sent him telegrams
almost hourly during the last ten days. Her final
message read: "I pray God spares your life. I embrace
you in my thought with all tenderness. Fight for your
life and for our love." He was buried temporarily in
Berlin, and six months later his body was sent to the
family plot in Mexico. The one million dollar estate
was left to Jaime's mother. Dolores Del Rio made no
claim against the estate.[12]

Shortly before Jaime's death, Dolores Del Rio confided
the reasons for the failure of her marriage to an interviewer: "At first Jaime was very much interested in my
career. That was when I was just beginning and not at
all important. But as soon as I had my first triumph,
his attitude changed. He was a typical Latin husband and
he had always known me as the submissive Latin wife. He
couldn't bear my success, and he hated being known as
"the husband of Dolores Del Rio." Latins are not accus-
tomed to this. They are brought up to think that they
are the masters, and they will not be anything else.
Their wives are only children. Why, the first thing a
Mexican man does when he marries is to take all his wife's
money away from her! What American would dare do this
to his wife!"

"When I first came here, I had been like a baby for so
many years, I couldn't even write a cheque! Jaime had
to take care of all my money. Now I do everything myself,
I won't have any help. I _love_ being like a man and man-
aging my own money."

"Then Jaime thought he would do some work of his own
that would bring him a success equal to mine. He started
to write and I was so glad because I thought he wouldn't

-33-

be jealous anymore and we would be happy again. But he
wrote script after script and didn't sell them, and he
blamed me for his failure."

Dolores reflected on her comments and then clarified
her interpretation: "As a mater of fact, it isn't a
question of nationality at all. The Latin husband and
the American husband are exactly the same when their dig-
nity and supremacy are threatened. I think the exception
would have to be a man who was just as important as his
wife, in some equally distinguished way. Someone so
sure of his own success that he would have no reason to be
jealous."13

As she reconsidered her married life, she realized
that her problems were not only of recent vintage. The
ten-year difference in age between Dolores and Jaime had
caused difficulties from the time of their courtship.
She confided her thoughts to an interviewer from Motion
Picture: "Immediately upon leaving the convent I became a
wife. I didn't know what love was. I didn't know what
marriage was. My husband was another kind friend who
told me what to do and how to do it. I loved him as a
child loves an older man who is kind to her, who takes
her places and gives her things, who knows more than she
does. My husband loved me as a man loves a child. He
did not love me as a man loves a woman."

"After my marriage I went into society. For a time I
thought that was fun. Compared to the life of the convent,
it was fun. I wore my first high-heeled shoes. I put
my hair up. I had grown-up gowns and jewels. I was
sixteen."

"I went to teas. I played a little bridge. I went to
dinner parties and receptions. I went as Mrs. Jaime Del
Rio and never, never as myself. I thought for a time I
was happy. That was because I had never known what
happiness is. Then I found out that I was dissatisfied,
restless."

"We went abroad. We lived in Paris, in Biarritz, all
over the Continent. I studied dancing in Paris and in
Spain. I studied the history of the arts. And I went to
parties...parties...parties. The best there are. So
many parties that now, at twenty-four, I have had too
many of them. I did everything there was to be done and--

-34-

it was not enough."

"After society, I had solitude. For a whole year we
lived among the Indians, with not a sign of white habita-
tion on the horizon, without the sight of a white face.
I learned service among the Indians. I learned the joy of
doing things for others, poorer and sadder than I."

"Still I was unsatisfied. Still I was not being myself.
That long lesson of patience became a crown of thorns to
me. I had not found myself and I could not be happy with--
a stranger."[14]

Despite Dolores Del Rio's harsh view of her married life
with Jaime, she was deeply affected by his death: "I
have had too much happen to me in too short a time. I
am twenty-four and I have been maid and wife, divorcee
and widow and actress. I have made money and I have known
success. I have lived in a dream and I have worked long
hours on end. I have known the greatest grief of my life-
the death of Jaime. Death had never come near to me
before. I had never experienced it. I shall never recover
from that scar. It is one of the scars that has made me
a woman."

When an interviewer asked Del Rio about her future
romantic plans, she cautiously replied: "Some day I hope
to find romance again. Love again. Not now. Now - for
a little time - I am done with love, I hope. I know it
is futile to make predictions about the emotions. I say
that I am done with them and, tomorrow, I may fall madly
in love and negate all that I have said today."

"But I hope to be free for a time - and one is never
free when one is in love. I have had too much, too much
of everything. I want a little while to breathe, to be
myself, to be free..."

"I have never known that great love of which the poets
sing. I believe there is such a thing, but I also
believe that it comes to only one person out of a million.
For the most part, I have found that we take what is at
hand. If a man is dying of thirst in the desert, he takes
what he can get to quench his thirst. It is so with us-
thirsty for love. I want freedom. I am going to get down
to life, whatever it may be."[15]

Although Dolores Del Rio's spirit seemed broken by the difficulties of her personal life, she continued appearing in films after Jaime's death. She seemed to bury her sorrows in hard work as she appeared in five films in 1928 and two in 1929. No Other Woman followed swiftly on the heels of Ramona. Dolores Del Rio portrayed Carmelita Desano, a South American heiress, in this 1928 film. Carmelita is courted by a wealthy Frenchman, but a crafty fortune hunter shatters the romance. The fortune hunter marries Carmelita himself, and immediately begins a spending spree. As Carmelita sees her fortune melting away, she returns to her first love, the Frenchman, who still remains true to her.

Dolores Del Rio was reunited with Raoul Walsh in her next film, The Red Dance. Walsh directed this story of revolutionary Russia which was based on Henry Leyford Gates' novel The Red Dancer Of Moscow. Del Rio, as the Russian peasant Tasia, is persuaded to assassinate the Grand Duke Eugen (Charles Farrell) on the eve of his marriage. The Duke is considered too liberal by members of the court and he must be eliminated. Tasia's shot misses the Duke, and she is gladdened since she has fallen in love with him. After the Revolution of 1917, Tasia becomes the famous Red Dancer of Moscow, and her lover, a former peasant, becomes General Ivan (Ivan Linow). Tasia discovers that the Duke is about to be killed by a firing squad. She begs Ivan to set him free, and the general agrees. Tasia and the Duke are thus united.

Revenge, directed by Edwin Carewe in 1928, featured Del Rio as Rascha, a gypsy woman. Jorga (LeRoy Mason), the lifelong enemy of Rascha's father, snips the young girl's braids. This is a sign of disgrace among the gypsies. Jorga feels remorse for his actions, and he sneaks into the gypsy camp late one evening and cuts off the braids of every woman. At the same time, he returns to Rascha her severed braids. As Jorga is leaving, Rascha awakes and begins to beat him. He grabs the whip from her hand and begins to kiss her. Jorga then kidnaps her and takes her to his secluded mountain retreat. He is determined to "tame" her, and she eventually falls in love with him. Rascha then helps her beloved Jorga escape the wrath of her father (James Marcus).

The Trail Of '98, Dolores Del Rio's first film for Metro-Goldwyn-Mayer, opened in 1929. While spoken dialogue had

-36-

been appearing in the latest sound films, Del Rio's
films remained mute. A musical score by David Mendoza
and William Axt was added to some prints of the film, and
a song "I Found Gold When I Found You" was also included.
Yet, the dialogue remained relegated to title cards in
this production.

Clarence Brown directed this film which was based on
the Robert William Service novel. The film is a brutal
depiction of the effect of gold on men and women during
the Alaskan gold rush. The lure of riches causes Samuel
Foote, known as "The Worm" (George Cooper), and Lars
Petersen (Karl Dane) to leave their homes and families
in search of easy wealth. The Bulkeys (Tenen Holtz and
Emily Fitzroy) move their restaurant to the Klondike in
order to profit from the newly rich miners. The Bulkeys
are accompanied by a poor relative, Berna (Dolores Del
Rio) and her blind grandfather (Cesare Gravina). He
unfortunately dies on the long trek to Alaska.

Berna meets Larry (Ralph Forbes), and they decide to
marry. But first Larry insists that he must search for
gold one more time. He joins with Lars, "The Worm", and
Jim (Tully Marshall) in this last search for wealth. "The
Worm" leaves Larry to die at the gold mine they have
discovered, but the evil "Worm" is eaten by wolves.
Larry returns to the local town and discovers that his
beloved Berna has become a prostitute. In anger Larry
burns down the saloon and kills the town's corrupt boss
Jack Locasto (Harry Carey). Larry, Berna, Lars, and Jim
take their new found wealth and attempt to rebuild their
shattered lives.

Evangeline, directed by Edwin Carewe, presented the
Mexican-American star as the Longfellow heroine. Evan-
geline lives with her father Benedict (Paul McAllister),
a farmer in the tiny Nova Scotian village of Grand-Pré.
Her father decides that she must marry Gabriel (Roland
Drew), son of Basil (James Marcus), the village smith.
Yet, she admires Baptiste (Donald Reed), the notary's son.
Before the marriage date France and England declare war.
The citizens, loyal to England, but with kinship ties to
France, refuse to join the battle. Britain orders the
men of the town deported, and the governor-general burns
the town to the ground. This action wounds Benedict,
who can no longer continue living once his home is de-
stroyed. He dies in Evangeline's arms.

Evangeline joins with Father Felician (Alec B. Francis)
on a thousand mile trek to Bayou Têche, Louisiana, new
home of the citizens of Grand Pré. Evangeline begins
her search for her beloved Gabriel. Baptiste, now a
wealthy land-owner, offers to marry Evangeline, but she
refuses. Evangeline wanders through the wilderness and
discovers a Jesuit mission. She becomes a Sister of
Mercy in the order, but she promises never to give up her
search for Gabriel. The Jesuits send Evangeline to
Philadelphia to care for the poor. At last, in an alms-
house, she finds her long-lost Gabriel.

Evangeline was Dolores Del Rio's last silent film.
Sound had transformed the motion picture industry, and
Del Rio had to follow this new trend or lose her popularity.

DOLORES DEL RIO   - 1919

DOLORES DEL RIO in "WHAT PRICE GLORY" (FOX) 1926

Roland Drew, Dolores Del Rio in "RAMONA"
UNITED ARTISTS - 1928

DOLORES DEL RIO - 1928

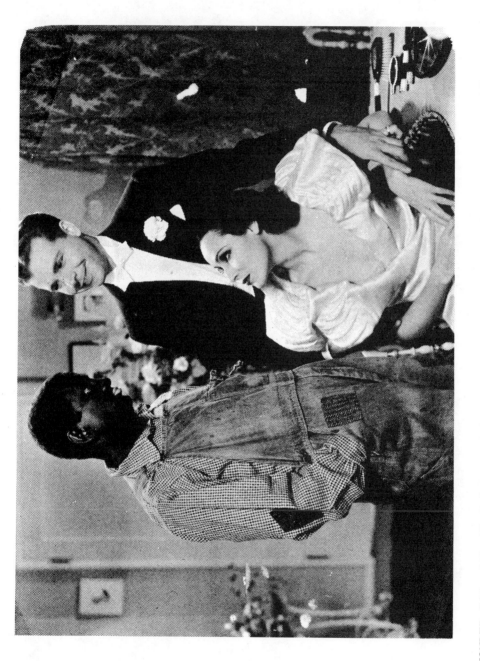

WONDER BAR with Al Jolson, Dick Powell and Dolores Del Rio — WARNER BROTHERS — 1934

Dolores Del Rio in MADAME DU BARRY - Warner Brothers - 1934

Dolores Del Rio, Warren William (in trunks) in WIDOW FROM MONTE CARLO - Warner Brothers - 1935

I LIVE FOR LOVE – Warner Brothers – 1935

From left to right: Everett Marshall, Allen Jenkins, Dolores Del Rio, Don Alvarado

DOLORES DEL RIO - 1937

James Leong, Dolores Del Rio, Dick Baldwin and June Lang in INTERNATIONAL SETTLEMENT 20TH. CENTURY-FOX (1938)

Dolores Del Rio and Jack Durant in JOURNEY INTO FEAR - RKO - 1942

Dolores Del Rio and Orson Welles in the Empire Room of the Waldorf-Astoria

Dolores Del Rio in THE FUGITIVE directed by John Ford - 1947

Dolores Del Rio and Elvis Presley in FLAMING STAR - 20TH. CENTURY-FOX - 1960

THE CHALLENGE OF SOUND: DOLORES DEL

RIO, 1930-1941

Motion pictures had never been totally silent.
From the first years of the film industry, the idea of
synchronized sound and motion pictures had fascinated
the inventors of the new cinematic art. By the 1920's
orchestral scores were routinely recorded on film. Yet,
dialogue remained absent from the screen.

Warner Brothers transformed the film industry with
the introduction of the Vitaphone process in 1926 with a
film version of the opera Don Juan. A year later, Al
Jolson's dynamic performance in Hollywood's first musical
comedy, The Jazz Singer, stunned film critics. When
Jolson told the audience, "Listen! you ain't heard nothin'
yet," dialogue became a permanent fixture on the American
screen.

Sound created new film personalities at the same
time as it destroyed the careers of such silent film
heroes as John Gilbert. Some stars adapted to the new
medium with ease, while others found themselves wholly
inadequate in the "talkies." Dolores Del Rio had three
years to make the transition to sound films. Fox added
an orchestral score to What Price Glory? in 1927, and
Ramona featured a title song. Yet, by 1930, the Mexican-
American actress still had not appeared in a film with
dialogue.

Dolores Del Rio dismissed the new "talkies" as a "passing fancy." She claimed that she resisted the sound films for artistic reasons, since she felt they would destroy "the movies which gave Hollywood its greatest work." Yet, as she made this comment in 1928, the fear lingered that she would be inadequate in the new medium. The silent film cloaked her voice in a veil of silence, while the "talkies" would reveal remnants of her Spanish accent.[1]

Producers urged her to appear in a sound film. They claimed that her accent was both "exotic" and "attractive." Del Rio responded that her accent was "terrible" and, "that was the end of the matter!" She confessed to an interviewer that her English was apt to desert her at crucial moments. It was this fear that delayed her first sound film until 1930.

Yet, by most accounts, Dolores Del Rio had mastered her second language with astonishing skill. When she first met Edwin Carewe in 1925 she was unable to speak a word of English. Her husband Jaime became the translator for the evening. By 1930, all but a trace of her Spanish accent had disappeared. As a result, she had little trouble with the English dialogue in her first sound films.

Although Dolores Del Rio made the transition to sound films with little difficulty, the remnants of her Spanish accent had other effects on her career. During the latter part of the silent era, she had escaped type casting as a Mexican or a Spaniard. She had appeared as a French woman in What Price Glory? and a Russian in Resurrection. Yet, with the introduction of sound to a formerly silent media, audiences were reminded of Del Rio's foreign heritage. As a result, she was forced to prove herself once again, as her first sound films returned her to the role of the sultry Spanish temptress. For the time being, the stereotype that Dolores Del Rio had seemingly escaped returned to haunt her.

The title of Dolores Del Rio's first all-talking picture, The Bad One, appeared ominous. Despite Dolores' ease with the English language, this United Artists' film became a commercial and critical flop. Dolores starred as Lita, a Spanish dancer, with Edmund Lowe, her co-star from What Price Glory?, who this time portrayed an American sailor.

-40-

Lita seduces Jerry Flanagan (Lowe) and causes him to jump ship. They eventually decide to wed, but an obstreperous Swede, Olaf Swenson, appears on their wedding day and claims the sultry Spanish dancer. Jerry and Olaf fight for Lita, and the Swede is killed in the ensuing battle. Lita testifies against Jerry at the trial, and the sailor is sentenced to prison. He refuses to see Lita from that day forward since he believes that she has deceived him.

Lita, however, still loves Jerry. She meets a prison guard named Pierre and promises to marry him. She has no feeling for the unwitting fellow, but hopes to use him in order to see Jerry. Jerry receives word of her plan, and urges Lita to resist, but Pierre intercepts the message. Meanwhile, the prisoners organize an escape attempt. Jerry discovers the plans and assumes leadership of the group. He leads the errant prisoners into a trap, and is awarded a pardon for his valiant deed. As the film ends, Jerry and Lita are reunited.

Despite the middling success of The Bad One at the box office, Dolores could still command a hefty $9000 a week salary from United Artists. Plans ensued for Dolores to appear in a remake of the 1928 Noah Berry and Norma Talmadge film The Dove. Yet, a variety of personal affairs threatened her career in the film industry. These events occurred with bizarre swiftness. In July, 1930, Dolores Del Rio was sued by her attorney, Gunther Lessing, for ruining his marriage. Lessing, who was also being sued by his own wife for divorce, claimed that Miss Del Rio "had described him to his wife as an ugly old man and had advised Mrs. Lessing to seek romance while she remained a young and beautiful girl." Mrs. Lessing denied these charges as did Dolores Del Rio: "Mr. Lessing's charges are false and malicious and are made in an attempt to embarrass me and collect money which is not due him. There is absolutely no foundation for his ridiculous statements."[2]

This affair had hardly calmed down when Dolores Del Rio announced her engagement to Cedric Gibbons, M-G-M art director, whom she had met at a Marion Davies party. Dolores Del Rio described her new conquest in a Photoplay interview:

> "Cedric is perfect," she asserted, and her eyes lighted up like burning candles.

"First, he is American, with that dash most American men seem to possess. And he is understanding and sympathetic. He has never been to Mexico and does not know my people--but he is an artist, and in his artist's appreciation he has been endowed with the sensitivity of the Latin. A perfect husband, no?"[3]

Dolores Del Rio planned to marry Cedric Gibbons on August 6, 1930. At first it seemed that the marriage might not be allowed. Shortly before the ceremony Father Augustine announced that he could not perform the wedding without a special dispensation since Del Rio had previously been married and divorced. The matter was swiftly resolved. Since Jaime had died after the divorce, Dolores needed only an authorization from her own church before the ceremony could take place. As a result, the marriage took place as scheduled in a quiet Franciscan mission, built in Santa Barbara in 1786.[4]

After the honeymoon, the new Mrs. Gibbons became seriously ill. This placed her hew United Artists contract in jeopardy. A clause provided that her arrangement with the studio would be nullified if she remained absent for more than one month for whatever reason. United Artists gave her an extra three days and then cancelled the contract.

Dolores recovered slowly from her illness, which many considered to be a nervous breakdown. Despite the loss of the UA contract, she soon returned to motion picture work. Her first effort was to be The Dove, newly retitled Girl Of The Rio by RKO studio heads.[5]

For a variety of reasons this was an unwise move. The original silent version of the film had been greeted harshly by critics and Latin American audiences. The sound version proved even more offensive. The theater which showed the film in Mexico City received continual threats of violence, and a special delegation visited Mexican President Ortiz Rubio to request immediate suspension of the film. The bitter resentment over Girl Of The Rio can be easily understood, since the film featured two prominent stars of Mexican heritage, Dolores Del Rio and Leo Carrillo, in unflattering roles. From the moment that Carrillo enters the Purple Pigeon Night Club, he appears as one of the most vile Mexicans yet portrayed on the screen.

Girl Of The Rio, directed by Herbert Brenon, is
situated in "Mexicana-just over the border," as the
title card explains. Señor Tostado (Carrillo) enters the
night club to the strains of Carmen and followed by a
flock of women. The oil-rich Tostado downs several drinks
and eyes the lovely Dolores (Del Rio), a singer in the
club. Tostado tells Dolores he loves her ("What I want,
I want"), but she resists his advances. She explains
that she already has a lover, Johnny Powell (Norman
Foster), who is "quick with a pistol." Dolores explains
to her friends: "I know what he wants, and what he wants
he cannot get!"

Tostado is not about to be thwarted in his love for
Dolores. He attempts to frame Johnny for the murder of a
peasant in a local gambling casino. Tostado later
arranges to have Johnny escape from jail and then shot in
the attempt.

Dolores begs Tostado to save Johnny's life. He re-
lents and exclaims that he "is the best damn caballero
in all Mexico." He allows Dolores to return to her
American lover.

This film revives many patterns that were formerly
seen only on the silent screen. Dolores prefers an
American to a Mexican lover. In a sense this is no surprise, since Tostado encapsulates the "greaser" image
that had formerly been purged from the screen. Yet,
once again, the Mexican male is portrayed as violent,
greedy, and lustful. Tostado's last minute conversion
hardly compensates for his behavior in the rest of the
film.

The claim that Tostado was the "best damn caballero
in all Mexico" so angered the Mexican Charge d'affaires
in Washington, D. C., that he requested the film be
banned in the United States. Panama and Nicaragua joined
with Mexico and refused to allow the film to enter their
borders.

Dolores Del Rio's second film for RKO whisks her
from the Mexican bordertown of Girl Of The Rio. Yet,
once again, she remains a foreigner who is hopelessly in
love with a North American male. This time she portrays
the lovely Polynesian Luana in Bird Of Paradise (1932).

-43-

Both King Vidor, the director, and David O. Selznick, head of production at RKO, despised the original stage version of Bird Of Paradise. Neither was able to finish reading the script. Selznick reported to Vidor: "I don't care what story you use as long as we call it Bird Of Paradise and Del Rio jumps into a flaming volcano at the finish." Vidor and screenwriter Wells Root left for Hawaii, where must of the film was shot, and fashioned a new story for Bird Of Paradise.[7]

Johnny Baker (Joel McCrea) discovers Luana swimming in a nearby stream and he falls in love with her. Although Luana does not understand English, she is a willing pupil. Soon she returns his affections. The elders of the village are upset by this turn of events, since they do not approve of the foreigner. The gods become angered by Johnny and Luana's courtship on forbidden ground. In order to appease the gods and Selznick, Luana dives into a volcano and the natural order is restored.

RKO followed Bird Of Paradise with a change of pace for Dolores. She was cast in a low budget musical, Flying Down To Rio, directed by Thorton Freedland. Although Dolores received star billing in the film, Flying Down To Rio is best remembered for the debut of Hollywood's foremost musical comedy team in the 1930's--Fred Astaire and Ginger Rogers. Billed fourth and fifth in the cast list, these two performers stole the film.

Yet this film is also of importance for Dolores Del Rio's career. In her first three sound films, she was bound by her accent into playing a foreigner of peasant birth. In Flying Down To Rio she abandons the rags of her previous roles and portrays the stunning Belinha de Rezende, a Brazilian heiress. Although she retains her Latin heritage in this film, she becomes an aristocrat. She could just as easily be French or Italian, since she is given none of the derogatory character traits that had been assigned to Latin women in other films.

Flying Down To Rio is remarkable not only for Miss Del Rio's role, but also for its portrayal of Latin American life in general. Rio de Janeiro is depicted as a bustling and modern metropolis rather than the provincial backwater seen in most films concerning Latin America. Indeed, it is a far cry from Rio's Road To Hell,(1932) which, as the title indicates, was hardly a flattering portrait of the Brazilian city. The Latin male, portrayed by Raul Roulien, is a sympathetic character. He is educated and sophisticated. Although he loses his beloved to Gene Raymond, he refuses to stand in the way of their happiness. In every way, Flying Down To Rio is a marked advance over Girl Of The Rio.

From the moment that Belinha de Rezende enters the Hotel Hibiscus nightclub, everyone is electrified by her beauty. She is even able to attract the handsome band leader, Roger Bond (Gene Raymond), from across a crowded dance floor by the mere flutter of an eyelash. This long distance flirtation so astonishes Belinha's North American chum (Mary Kornman), that she comments, "What have these South Americans got below the equator that we haven't?"

Belinha should not be trying to attract Roger since she is currently engaged to Julio Rubeiro (Raul Roulien). Nevertheless, Roger is unable to resist her charms, and he offers to fly her to Rio de Janeiro in his own plane. She accepts despite the reservations of her guardian.

Roger flies Belinha to Rio where he discovers that her father owns the hotel in which the band is booked. This would seem to provide a basis for the continuation of the romance, but three sinister Greeks wish the hotel to fail. As a result, the Hotel Atlantico is denied an entertainment license and Roger's band cannot perform.

The perspicacious Roger discovers a solution to this messy dilemma. Since the Brazilian government has no control over the space above the hotel, Roger designs an air show to end all air shows. The chorus girls don flying garb, attach their shoes to the wings of several small biplanes, and present their musical number in the skies of Rio. Naturally, the song is "Flying Down To Rio."

Roger's machinations save the hotel, and he decides to marry Belinha. Julio discovers that Belinha really loves Roger, so he decides to bow out gracefully. As he and Belinha fly away to be married, he dons a parachute and jumps from the airplane, leaving Belinha alone with Roger as the film ends.

Only one scene mars the generally sensitive portrayal of Latin American life. The Carioca dance number, performed by whites, the second by mulattoes--and the third by Blacks. Each racial group leaves the stage as the next appears. This racial segregation is less reflective of

Brazil than of North America. Arlene Croce suggests in The
Fred Astaire and Ginger Rogers Book a kinder motive for
this racial segregation. She argues that Art Director
Van Nest Polgase used Flying Down To Rio as an opportunity
to play with the variety of shades between white and black.
Ginger Rogers is constantly juxtaposed with Raul Roulien,
and the blond Gene Raymond continually appears next to the
dusky Dolores Del Rio.[8] This may be the case, but the
separation of dancers by race seems a characteristic of
the Hollywood mind rather than racially mixed Brazilian
society.

By 1934 Dolores Del Rio's career seemed to have
returned to the heights she had known during the silent
era. Yet, a minor incident threatened her success. In
mid-1934 Los Angeles District Attorney Neil McAllister
began an investigation of Communist influence in Hollywood. The names of Lupe Velez, Ramón Novarro, James
Cagney, and Dolores Del Rio were found on a sheet of paper
belonging to Caroline Decker, secretary of the Cannery
and Agricultural Workers Union, which had been named a
"Communist Organization." These Hollywood stars had supposedly contributed to this Union's activities.

Each star staunchly denied the accusations. Cagney
replied that "he was against all 'isms' except American-
ism. He viewed McAllister's actions as a mere publicity
stunt in an election year.

The remaining performers, all of Latin American
descent, were similarly shocked and angered by the charges.
Lupe Velez shouted: "Me a Communist? Ho, I don't know
what the blazes a Communist is. I'm not so dumb that I
would have anything to do with something that I don't know
what it is." Novarro agreed with Velez, although his
response sounded considerably more cogent: "We give money
to needy people--crippled people on the streets who ask us
for a quarter for something to eat. But we have never
given money to any Communist or any similar organization."

Cedric Gibbons presented a similar denial for Dolores
Del Rio: "My wife has no connection with the Communist
movement. She is not interested in radical activities
and has never contributed funds to the Communists or any
similar organization."

The investigation was swiftly dropped and it had
little effect on these stars' careers in 1934. Yet, these
charges did not die easily. For example, Cagney claims

that he portrayed George M. Cohan, the "damnedest patriotic man in the whole world" in <u>Yankee</u> <u>Doodle</u> <u>Dandy</u> in order to quiet doubts about his loyalty to the American government. The ramifications for Dolores Del Rio were of somewhat greater import. Almost twenty years later she applied for a visa to re-enter the United States in order to appear in the film <u>Broken</u> <u>Lance</u>. In the atmosphere of the McCarthy years, McAllister's charges were recalled, and Del Rio was denied entry into the country.

Yet, in the 1930's, the McAllister investigation had little effect on her film career. After <u>Flying</u> <u>Down</u> <u>To</u> <u>Rio</u> Dolores Del Rio signed a contract with Warner Brothers. <u>Wonder</u> <u>Bar,</u> her first film with her new studio, reduced her to a featured player for the time being. This new musical featured Al Jolson, Kay Francis, Dick Powell and Ricardo Cortez and six new songs by Harry Warren and Al Dubin. Lloyd Bacon directed the film and Busby Berkeley choreographed the musical sequences. As a result, Dolores Del Rio almost got lost in the shuffle.

<u>Wonder</u> <u>Bar</u> is a musical tale of unrequited love. Al Wonder, (Al Jolson) host of the famous London night spot, is in love with the lead dancer Ynez (Dolores Del Rio). She is also loved by Tommy (Dick Powell), the young singer at the Wonder Bar. Ynez, at first, cares for neither of them. She prefers her dancing partner Harry (Ricardo Cortez). Harry, meanwhile, desires the rich socialite Liane Renaud (Kay Francis). Lest everyone remain unsatisfied by the end of the film, Ynez realizes that Harry is a two-timer and stabs him. She accepts Tommy, and Al Wonder, always a gentleman, steps aside. The stabbing is hushed up, and Ynez and Tommy are free to marry.

Amidst these plot machinations, Dolores Del Rio appeared in a fantastic Tango number with Ricardo Cortez. After the dance, the camera pulls backward. Del Rio and Cortez remain small dots on the night club seen from the high ceiling of the Wonder Bar. Busby Berkeley describes the conclusion of the number: "I had them build me sixty tall white movable columns, to move against a black background. The columns were on separate tracks, independent of each other and all controlled ectrically. I had a hundred dancers dance with the columns. Then they all disappeared and in their place was a huge forest of silver trees with a white reindeer running around. To get the effect I wanted, I built an octagon of mirrors, each twenty-eight feet high and twelve feet wide and inside this octad a revolving platform twenty-four feet in diameter."

"When I was drawing up my plans for this, everyone at the studio thought I had lost my mind. Even Sol Polito, one of the best cameramen I ever worked with, couldn't figure out how I was going to photograph a production from inside without the camera being seen. Actually, when I figured it out in my office using eight little compacts-- the kind girls carry in their handbags--I discovered there was a way of moving at the center of the mirrors without being reflected."9

At the end of the scene, the camera returns to two masked dancers. The masks fall to the ground revealing Dolores and Ricardo. She exclaims breathlessly, "Why can't this go on forever?" The night club audience then applauds wildly.

This film had little time to be critical of Latin sterotypes since Busby Berkeley and Al Jolson concentrated on Negro images in "Going To Heaven On A Mule," perhaps the most racist musical number ever seen on film. Jolson, in blackface, rides to heaven on a mule. He discovers a huge watermelon. It begins to open and five black tap-dancers emerge from within. They are eating fried chicken as they perform. The number declines swiftly from that low point.

Dolores Del Rio served her apprenticeship at Warners with Wonder Bar. She followed that film with her first full fledged starring role in Madame DuBarry in 1934. Although several scenes were eliminated by censors, she dominated the screen as never before.

Louis XV (Reginald Owen) is bored. Every woman he desires is either too respectful or involved in a palace intrigue. Richelieu (Osgood Perkins) discovers Du Barry (Del Rio) and views her as an ideal woman for the King. Louis returns to his carriage and discovers Du Barry. He is enraptured and vows to do whatever she wishes. He dons her shoes and even makes her breakfast, his famous omelettes d'amour.

Du Barry is unsatisfied with the king's gifts. She wants him to prove that he loves her by taking her sleigh-riding on a summer day. The king dumps the problem in the laps of his lackies. They pour tons of salt in the palace courtyard, and Du Barry and Louis ride in the "snow". Yet,

Du Barry is unsatisfied. She commands Louis to make his
ten-year old Negro servant a governor of a province.
Louis is shocked by the idea:
    Louis: Madame, what are you doing to France?
    Du Barry: Just what it is doing to me!

Nevertheless, he agrees to her whim and loves her all the
more for it. Six months later, when it actually snows,
Louis invites Du Barry for another sleigh ride in the
courtyard. "I don't like real snow," she replies.

    D'Aiguillon (Victor Jory) arrives at the palace
and explains to Louis that discontent is rampant through-
out the realm: "You're losing your kingdom. Millions
are starving. Yet you give fabulous jewels to Du Barry.
There is treason everywhere. Why should this woman control
the destiny of France?" Louis replies, "She makes me forget that I am nearly sixty."

    Du Barry enters and is introduced to D'Aiguillon.
He comments, "I met Madame a long time ago--at a house."
Du Barry clarifies his statement: "A gambling house."
She has heard D'Aiguillon's complaints to the king, so
she gives him her jewels. "Sell them--give the money to
whoever needs it." D'Aiguillon replies: "I will take the
money back to where it came from."

    Du Barry's scandalous actions continue to shock the
Royal Court. She appears in a nightgown before the
assembled royalty. Louis appears offended and stalks from
the room. He then peeps from behind the door and motions
to Du Barry to follow him to the royal bedroom.

    Du Barry's bliss is upset by the arrival of young
Marie Antoinette (Anita Louise) who is to marry the young
Dauphin (Maynard Holmes). Louis requests Du Barry to explain the facts of life to the dim-witted Dauphin. Antoinette discovers Du Barry in the bedroom of her intended.
Although no indiscretion has been committed, a fight en-
sues between the women of the palace. Louis is distrubed
by the commotion and suffers a heart attack.

    Du Barry goes to Louis' bedside. He claims that he
does not mind dying since he enjoyed the years with Du
Barry so much. The king dies as he laments the fate of
poor France under the rule of his son who will become
Louis XVI.

Marie Antoinette, who has never liked Du Barry, urges the new king to imprison his father's mistress. Du Barry greets the news stoically: "Oh well, it is so much better than being hung." As she leaves the palace with her guards she spots Louis and Marie. She bows before them and states: "Farewell, I've had such a nice time." She then grabs the arms of her guards and sticks her tongue out at the astonished Marie Antoinette. She leaves the palace as she sings Louis' favorite folk song.

In Caliente (1935) returned Dolores Del Rio to a south of the border setting and reunited her with Leo Carrillo, her co-star in Girl Of The Rio. The passing of a few years had brought few changes in the attitudes toward Latins. Yet, Dolores Del Rio escapes unscathed. She remains the beautiful leading lady, and is never the target of ethnic slurs. Leo Carrillo, however, portrays José Gómez, a gentleman with a penchant for cards and gambling. Harold Brandon (Edward Everett Horton) is less kind. He comments, "He calls himself Gómez--it is probably Mexican for Jesse James." The inhabitants of Caliente are depicted as bumbling locals. The townspeople are unable to speak English unless they are bribed. This gag is repeated four times in the film.

Dolores Del Rio portrays Rita Gómez, the famous dancer known as La Españita. She is weary after an international tour, so she visits a health spa in the border town of Caliente. Larry MacArthur (Pat O'Brien) also arrives in Caliente to escape the clutches of a designing blonde. As entertainment critic for a New York newspaper, he has reviewed La Españita's latest performance and panned it unmercifully. Unfortunately, he was too busy to see the performance, so he concocted an unfavorable review.

Rita discovers Larry's identity and vows to take revenge for his critical review. She pretends she loves him, and at the last moment she plans to leave him. Yet, after a short period, she is unable to control her emotions, and she falls for Larry. She performs "Muchacha" ("Muchacha, tonight I gotcha where I wantcha") for Larry and he is decidedly impressed. He realizes her true identity and after several Busby Berkeley dance numbers, they decide to wed.

I Live For Love was Dolores Del Rio's third motion picture with Busby Berkeley. Although he directed the

entire film it remained remarkably calm, displaying little
of the choreographic pyrotechnics that ignite his earlier
films. Nevertheless, I Live For Love showed that Busby
Berkeley had a flair for quick dialogue and intimate
comedies.

The film opens as the entire city heads to work.
Amid the garbage men and the construction workers, cacoph-
ony reigns. Suddenly a street singer arrives. He begins
to sing and passersby stop to listen, and the workers
stop their noise. In the crowd are the producers of a
new Broadway show. They have a dilemna. Their star,
Donna Alverez (Del Rio), who "is South America's greatest actress," has selected a two-bit gigolo for her co-
star in her new show. Rico (Don Alvarado) has flattered
Donna so, that she insists on performing with him. The
producers try to substitute the street singer Roger Kerry
(Everett Marshall) for Rico.

Donna refuses to perform with Kerry since she claims
he cannot act. Kerry replies: "I will never be your
leading man. Take Rico! Two bad actors--you'll be great
together." She stalks from the stage and he leaves the
theater. The incident is picked up by the newspapers
("Street Singer Spurns Lead Role") and Kerry becomes
famous. A soap company offers him a weekly radio show.

Unwittingly, Donna is booked on Kerry's show, and from
the moment she sees him their tempers flare. Donna insists
on appearing first since she has a performance later that
evening. "There are one thousand people at the theater
waiting for me to act." Kerry replies, "And there are six
million people waiting for me to sing." Roger appears
first and sings "I Live For Love." He then introduces
Donna, but pretends to forget her name. She thanks him,
and also pretends to forget his. She leaves the radio
studio hoping to leave the nightmare behind her.

Roger follows Donna to the theater and attends the
the premiere of her new play, a drama about ancient Greece.
Kerry hears the audience grumble about Rico's performance
("Who ever heard of a Greek with a moustache?"), and delays
taking his orchestra seat until the middle of the first
act. The repeated "pardon me's" disturb Donna's performance. She sheds her role and comes to center stage: "If
you are quite comfortable Mr. Kerry, may I go on with the
play?"

Roger buys Donna flowers in order to apologize.
She refuses to talk to him. Yet, the next morning, she
discovers an article in a gossip column: "Royal Romance
Revealed." Although her own agents placed the story,
Donna believes that once again it is Roger's doing. He
again tries to talk to her, but she refuses.

After Donna's show closes, the fights continue.
Yet, their personalities begin to soften. Roger sings
his favorite ballad for Donna and she succumbs, although
the reason for Donna's conversion is not made clear in
the screen play. They decide to marry almost immediately.
They also vow to give up their careers ("It's either our
careers or our happiness") and retire.

The marriage plans please everyone except Donna's
agents. They pretend that she has been offered a play
"by America's greatest playwright." She decides to appear
on Broadway again and Roger breaks the engagement. The
crafty agents even return Rico to the scene. Donna,
lonely and unhappy, decides to marry him. On the day of
the wedding Roger returns. Donna leaves Rico at the altar
and jumps into Roger's car. They kiss as the film ends.
Once again the North American has conquered a Latin rival
in the game of love.

   Widow From Monte Carlo, Dolores Del Rio's last film
for Warner Brothers in the 1930's, presents Dolores as a
"grieving" widow who suddenly appears at the gambling
tables in Monte Carlo. Dressed entirely in black, the
Duchess Inez (Del Rio) reveals a penchant for dice.
Major Allan Chepstoe (Warren William) notices her ("Are
you by any chance an international spy?") and bets his
fortune on the Duchess' age (24). He wins and turns to
kiss the mysterious woman. She immediately leaves the
casino.

The Duchess Inez returns to her room to meet the
questions of her inquisitive guardians, relatives of the
late Duke. Although she has remained in mourning for a
year, the relatives are not satisfied. They fear she will
embarrass Eric (Colin Clive), whom they have selected for
her next husband. Inez calms their fears: "I wore a veil.
No one recognized me. Not even the man who kissed me."
Eric is somewhat startled by this revelation, but he is
calmed by the Duke's cousin: "These Latin women are like
that--impetuous, fiery--you should marry her while she's
in the mood." The young man follows his cousin's advice.

Eric attempts to propose, but he is unable to find the
proper words: "A strong bond of affection has grown up
between us--haven't you noticed?" Inez accepts the pro-
posal, but Eric does not kiss her. She asks, "Do you
think kissing is vulgar? I think it is fun." It hardly
seems an auspicious start for a courtship.

Inez meets Allan once again in Cannes. He tells
her of the glories of a London amusement park, then kisses
her, and leaves. When Inez returns to London she finds
a note from Allan asking her to join him at the park.
She agrees, but insists that they return that evening so
no one will miss her. They have a delightful time, and
Allan asks her to join him again. She refuses, reminding
her escort that she is engaged. "Do you love him?" he
asks. "Let's not talk about it," answers Inez.

Inez writes Allan that she will never forget the
night they spent together, but she can no longer see him
because she and Eric have announced their engagement.
Allan's social-climbing neighbor Mrs. Torrent (Louise
Fazenda) steals the letter and threatens to blackmail the
Duchess. If Inez does not attend Mrs. Torrent's party on
Saturday night she will reveal the contents of the letter
to Eric.

Inez vows to spare Eric the pain the letter would
cause and she resolves to break the engagement: "I agreed
to marry for family's sake, but we will never be happy.
Our marriage would spoil our friendship. Let's at least
keep that."

In the meantime Allan discovers the letter and returns
it to Inez. They decide to marry and they take a cruise
to Canada, their future home.

Dolores Del Rio's contract lapsed after two disappointing films. She left Warners and became a free agent appearing in motion pictures for a variety of studios. United
Artists released Accused, Dolores Del Rio's first British
film, in 1936. She appeared with Douglas Fairbanks, Jr.
in this minor murder mystery. While Del Rio received slight
praise for her performance, the New York Times harshly
criticized Fairbanks: "As producer, Mr. Fairbanks really
should insist that his technicians come abreast of the
times and master such rudiments of picturemaking as proper

lighting, set construction, and sound recording. The
performances were worthy of more charitable handling."[10]

Devil's Playground, released in 1937 by Columbia,
continued Del Rio's string of unexceptional films. The
Times once again damned with faint praise: "It is a motion picture with a completely commonplace idea--a story
of two petty officers, a dancing girl, and a submarine
mishap--treated with the detailed care and technical
respect of a Hollywood superspecial. It is, in short, B
product at its unimportant best."[11]

Actually, Devil's Playground resembles an under-
water version of What Price Glory? The Liam O'Flaherty,
Jerome Chorodov, and Dalton Trumbo screenplay presents
two bosom buddies who fall in love with the same woman.
Jack Dorgan (Richard Dix) portrays the navy's champion
diver, while friend Robert Mason (Chester Morris) is an
expert on submarine warfare. Carmen (Dolores Del Rio)
tries to trap Dorgan into marriage at the same time as
she flirts with Mason. Mason discovers that Carmen is
engaged to his friend, so he leaves nobly, without dis-
closing the woman's actions. Dorgan comes to the rescue
of a trapped submarine, and saves his friend's life.
Carmen realizes the true friendship of Dorgan and Mason,
and decides to leave.

Lancer Spy (1937), directed by Gregory Ratoff,
featured the young George Sanders in his first major screen
role. Sanders portrayed a dashing naval officer who is
chosen the the British Intelligence Service to impersonate
a German nobleman. The "nobleman" is allowed to return
to Germany, and, in the person of George Sanders, discover
information of vital importance to the war effort.

International Settlement (1938) followed soon after,
and once again George Sanders dominated the film, although
Dolores Del Rio maintained star billing. While the film
was primarily a melodrama of life in Shanghai, Twentieth-
Century-Fox gave the screenplay a topical turn by adding
newsreel footage which explained the importance of China
to the war raging in Asia. New York Times found International Settlement a disaster: "With the exception of the
bombs, the first of which explodes just as the plot is
about to, the only difference between "International Settlement" and the average Occidental melodrama is the fact that
people drive up to sinister buildings in rickshas instead
of taxicabs. The comedy, if anything, is much worse for

the voyage--such drolleries as June Lang learning to use
chopsticks, or getting cutely intoxicated on rice wine,
without disarranging a single hair of her remarkable
permanent." The only compliment was reserved for Dolores
Del Rio: "It is true that the film might have been a
great deal worse: the glamorous lady might not have been
Dolores Del Rio, in which case her glamour would have been
reduced by half."[12]

The Man From Dakota, released by Metro-Goldwyn-
Mayer, continued Dolores Del Rio's string of undistinguish-
ed films in the late 1930's. The film is based on Mac
Kinlay Cantor's novel Arouse and Beware, a Civil War tale
of two Union prisoners who escape from Confederate clutches
and travel north to bring important information to General
Grant. While this might have been an exciting adventure
film, the New York Times noted that it had "been turned
into a proper Sunday school picnic with comic overtones."[13]
Wallace Beery's comic mugging once again gave Dolores Del
Rio little opportunity to perform.

After Del Rio had completed The Man From Dakota,
her personal life began to crumble. Her blissful marriage
to Cedric Gibbons in 1930 became bitter a decade later.
There were hints of tension as early as 1938. B. R.
Crisler noted in the New York Times that Cedric Gibbons
had prohibited interviews with his famous wife on their
upcoming New York trip:

> The news had already preceded the Gibbons party that
> Miss Del Rio was not to be interviewed this trip.
> Before leaving the Coast, we were informed, Mr.
> Gibbons had exacted from his famous wife the promise
> that she would not annoy him by cluttering up the
> hotel with newspaper people. Life is too short,
> Mr. Gibbons has declared, to waste on interviews,
> and Miss Del Rio, the fiery Latin, an international
> spy, the cinematic femme fatale, had mousily acqui-
> esced.[14]

By 1940, the tensions became unbearable and the
Gibbons separated in March of that year. As Del Rio
parted for Palm Springs, she told reporters that she and
her husband had not yet thought about divorce nor had
they found new romantic interests. She explained the
separation in a rational manner: "We simply decided that
our marriage had become impossible, and when that happens
to two people I think it is best to part."[15]

By January of the following year, divorce appeared
inevitable. Accompanied by her friend Fay Wray, she told
Superior Judge Thurmond Clarke that Gibbons' "cold and
indifferent" attitude made her nervous and ill. Wray
agreed with Del Rio's observations noting that she had
"observed Mr. Gibbons' cruel and indifferent attitude
during frequent visits to the couple's home." This is
not to say that Gibbons actually was "cruel and indifferent"
to Miss Del Rio. These remarks were more than likely a
response to California's divorce laws. Yet, whatever
the precise reasons, the divorce was granted on January 17,
1941. Soon afterwards, Dolores Del Rio began dating
Hollywood's young genius, Orson Welles, who cast her in
his new film Journey Into Fear.

Journey Into Fear, based on an Eric Ambler novel,
is set in Istanbul during the turbulent period at the
beginning of the Second World War. Howard Graham (Joseph
Cotton), an American engineer, meets his company's local
representative Kopelkin (Everett Sloane) and they decide
to attend a local club. An ominous fat man follows the
duo to their destination.

The boite has two featured acts. The first stars
Josette Martel (Dolores Del Rio) and her dancing boys.
Josette enters, dressed as a feline, and attempts to
seduce the hesitant Graham. She completes her song and
is followed on the bill by a magician (Han Conried).
The magician drags the unwilling Graham to the stage as
his assistant. He swiftly ties Graham's hands and feet
to the wall. Suddenly, the lights go out and a shot is
heard. The lights return and the magician is found dead
bound to the wall in the same place that Graham had been.
Had the shot occurred a moment sooner, Graham would have
been the victim.

The Turkish police arrive almost immediately, and
hustle everyone in the club to jail. Colonel Haki (Orson
Welles) arrives, and summons Graham into his office.
Haki knows every detail about the American's life. He
knows that Graham possesses naval intelligence secrets,
and that the Nazis are intending to capture or to kill
him. Haki advises Graham to change his travel plans. He
strongly urges him to travel by cattle boat over the Black
Sea instead of taking the land route as he had originally
planned. As he prepares to board the ship, Kopelkin slips
him a gun for his own protection.

As Graham climbs the gangplank, he meets the dancer
Josette. She is surprised to see him, since the night
before he had said that he was traveling by train.

Josette: Tell me truthfully why you're on this boat.
Graham: Someone is trying to kill me.
Josette: Don't joke about such things! I am
          from the Pyrennes. My parents were very
          poor. I tell you the truth. Why do
          you not tell me the truth?

Despite Graham's reticence, Josette becomes friendly with him. She confides that she despises her dance
partner, and warns Graham to be careful of him. Graham
hardly needs a warning to be careful of those on ship-
board. Virtually everyone appears suspicious to him in
one way or another. Yet, these fears pale as Graham
discovers that the fat man, Banat (Jack Moss) is also
aboard ship, Graham runs to the ship's captain and asks
to be put ashore. The captain laughs at his fears,
denies the request, and returns to a deep sleep.

Graham explains his desperate situation to Josette.
This time she believes him and volunteers to stall Banat
while Graham searches his stateroom. Graham first
returns to his own room and discovers that his gun has been
stolen. He is without protection. Yet it is to no
avail. The real villain, Mueller, has been aboard the
ship for the entire voyage posing as a timid archaeologist.
Banat has been following his orders since the Istanbul
murder. Mueller discusses Graham's demise in a calm
manner. Graham has two choices: he may be shot as the
ship docks the next morning or he may be injected with
typhus germs and remain in a hospital bed for the next
six weeks. The latter option, explains Mueller, would be
less messy. The six week "rest" would delay the latest
naval secrets from reaching the Allies, time enough for the
Nazis to gain the advantage. Graham is given until the
next morning to make his decision.

Fortunately, Graham is not alone. A secret agent for
Haki, Kuvetli (Edgar Barrier), reveals that he has over-
heard the conversation. They attempt to devise a scheme
to foil Mueller's plans, but it is to no avail. Barely an
hour later, Kuvetli is discovered shot to death. Graham
panics and foresees no escape. Yet, he has the foresight
to ask a fellow voyager to phone Haki as soon as the ship
docks. The passenger agrees and gives Graham a tiny pen
knife. It is hardly a weapon, but, by this time, Graham
will accept any help he can get.

Mueller and Banat escort Graham down the gangplank
where they are met by an automobile and two well-armed
thugs. As the automobile weaves through the twisted
streets of the Turkish city, a tire suddenly explodes.
Graham seizes the opportunity, and drives his pen knife
into the car's horn. The noise both attracts considerable
attention from the crowd and causes confusion within the
car. Graham grabs the wheel from the distracted driver
and steers the auto into a store window. Graham then leaps
from the car and escapes into the crowd.

Graham foolishly returns to the hotel where his
wife Stephanie (Ruth Warrick) is staying. Mueller and
Banat assumed Graham would flee to the hotel, so they
arrive early and explain to the wife that they are business
associates who wish to speak with Mr. Graham. Graham
discovers the two Nazis in his room and dismisses his wife
to the bar so he may "discuss business with the gentlemen."
Actually, he does not want his wife to be hurt in the
seemingly inevitable gunfight.

After Stephanie leaves, Mueller explains that he has
no more time to waste--Graham must be killed. Mueller
leaves the apartment, and tells Banat to do away with
Graham. As Banat is about to shoot, the telephone rings.
Josette has called to inquire about his health. During
this brief respite Graham distracts Banat and jumps onto
the ledge outside his apartment. Colonel Haki arrives
shortly thereafter and shoots Mueller. The driving rain
blinds the fat man and he falls from the hotel ledge. The
ordeal is over, and the Grahams may return to their normal
life.

After Journey Into Fear was completed, Dolores Del
Rio's romance with Orson Welles ended abruptly. He began
seeing Rita Hayworth, who would soon appear in his film
The Lady From Shanghai. With her film career drifting,
Dolores Del Rio decided to return to Mexico to recover
from her recent divorce. She sold her Hollywood mansion
and bought a villa in Coyoacan, which is near Mexico City.
Yet, she did not remain absent from the screen for long.
Her native country Mexico became the scene of her greatest
triumphs. Within a few years, she would become the first
lady of the Mexican cinema.

V. DEL RIO IN MEXICO

When Dolores Del Rio arrived in Mexico, the film
industry still remained in its infancy. Although a few
Mexican films had received international acclaim, most
domestic motion pictures were inexpensive copies of the
Hollywood product.

While the production of films in Mexico began at
almost the same time as in the United States, lack of
funds and technology limited the development of this
Latin American cinema. Salvador Toscano Barragán imported
the first projector from France and opened the first movie
theater in Mexico in 1896. By 1916, the nation's first
production company, Mexico-Lux, began the first feature
length silent films. Although the transition to sound
caught Mexican film-makers unawares, producers adapted
to the new medium rather quickly. In 1930, the first
sound film was produced in Mexico.[1]

The Depression halted the rapid growth of the Mexican
film industry. While the 1930's became the golden era for
Hollywood, Mexican film production stagnated. It became
more profitable to import American, European, or Argentine
films than to produce films domestically.[2]

Ironically, the coming of World War II aided the Mexican film industry. It became more difficult for Mexico

to import European motion pictures, and at the same time,
the Argentine film industry was unable to maintain a suf-
ficient supply of film stock. As a result, by the time
the war began, Mexico became the primary producer of Spanish
language films.

The fact that Dolores Del Rio began her Mexican film
career during this boom period was one of the major reasons
for her outstanding success. Films could at last compete
technologically with foreign rivals. The second factor of
Del Rio's success was her ability to recognize talent.
Within a year of her return to Mexico, she had assembled
a repertory group of the top creative talents in the Mexican film industry. Together, this team brought fame and
renown to the budding Mexican cinema.

Del Rio's ensemble consisted of a director, a lead
actor, and a photographer. Through cooperation this group
created some of Mexico's best remembered films. Emilio
Fernández, known as "El Indio," directed and supplied the
screenplay for many Del Rio films. Until 1941, he was
primarily known as an actor, a career to which he would
occasionally return. In that year he directed <u>La Isla de
la Pasión</u> ("The Island of Passion") with David Silva,
Isabela Corona, and Pedro Armendáriz. In the following
year he directed <u>Soy Puro Mexicano</u>, also with Silva and
Armendáriz. Despite some favorable comment, Fernández
would not receive acclaim until he began to work with
Dolores Del Rio.

Gabriel Figueroa, the second member of the Del Rio
team, provided the photography. Figueroa had become one
of the most honored of Mexican cameramen. Often his photography could embellish a second-rate script and provide
considerable interest for film audiences. Virtually every
film he has photographed has been honored by Mexican and
international critics. Figueroa studied photography both
in Mexico and in Hollywood. Gregg Toland, who photographed
<u>Citizen Kane</u>, became his mentor in the film capital.
Figueroa returned to Mexico in 1936 and photographed <u>Allá
en el Rancho Grande</u> and <u>Jalisco Nunca Pierde</u> ("Jalisco
Never Loses"). Both films immediately won high praise.[2]

Pedro Armendáriz, the leading actor in many Del Rio
films, became the fourth member of this talented quartet.
Armendáriz made his debut in the 1935 film <u>María Elena</u>,
directed by Raphael J. Sevilla. The twenty-three year old
actor won high praise for his performance as a sailor in

this film. Interestingly, the cast list reveals that Emilio Fernández also portrayed a dancer in <u>María Elena</u>. After appearing in <u>Rosario</u> in the same year, Armendáriz was in great demand. In 1937, he co-starred in <u>Jalisco Nunca Pierde</u>, photographed by Gabriel Figueroa, who would also join the Del Rio repertory. By 1943, Armendáriz became one of the most popular actors in Mexico.

Del Rio, Fernández, Figueroa, and Armendáriz helped to transform the Mexican cinema. All too often, Mexican films had attempted to copy Hollywood product. This talented team turned its attention to the Mexican reality. Mexican historical themes were emphasized in the scripts as were the problems of the Mexican peasantry. Figueroa began to explore the Mexican landscape and integrate it into his films. Del Rio and Armendáriz concerned themselves with the lives and emotions of Mexico's humble classes rather than the wealthy aristocrats who had populated the Mexican screen. This new focus on the Mexican nation caused critics to compare these cinematic creations to the art of Orozco, Siqueiros, and Rivera.

Dolores Del Rio began <u>Flor Silvestre</u>, her first Mexican film, in January 1943. Directed by Emilio Fernández, this folk tale of the Mexican Revolution won the actress high praise for her first Spanish language acting performance.

<u>Flor Silvestre</u>, based on the novel <u>Sucedió Ayer</u> by Fernando Robles, depicts the class struggle in Mexico after the overthrow of Porfirio Diaz in 1911. An elderly peasant woman, Esperanza (Del Rio) tells her young son the history of the Castro family, formerly the wealthiest landowners in the valley. As a flashback begins, Esperanza explains that she was once engaged to José Luis (Pedro Armendáriz), the Castro family heir. The patriarch Don Francisco Castro (Miguel Angel Ferriz) discovers that his son is not only courting a peasant girl, but also flirting with revolutionary politics. As a result, he banishes José Luis from the family estate.

José Luis disobeys his father's wishes and lives with Esperanza although they are unmarried. Their lives are happy, especially after José's political party triumphs in the post-revolutionary elections. Yet, José remains estranged from his family.

-61-

José Luis discovers that two bandits, posing as revolutionaries, have seized his father's ranch. Fernando resists the thieves, so they hang the elderly gentleman. Eager for revenge, José returns to his family estate and hangs the bandit Ursulo. Ursulo's partner, Rogelio, is eager to escape a similar fate, so he kidnaps Esperanza and her newly born son. If José does not abandon his quest, Rogelio vows to massacre his family. José cannot allow his wife and child to be killed, so he surrenders. Rogelio then murders José, as his wife and son watch.[4]

Flor Silvestre was released in a subtitled version for a short time in the United States. It allowed North American audiences to view the former Hollywood star in a Mexican film. The North American reviewers were uniformly harsh to this maiden effort. The New York Times commented: "Although the picture only runs an hour and thirty minutes-this is a decided improvement over the usual two hours-plus length of Mexican productions-it has been directed at such a slow pace that it fails to hold interest...The trouble is that the picture makes the audience suffer her [Esperanza's] every hardship, which struck us as carrying things too far, especially since the revolution is depicted in more or less comic-opera fashion. Miss Del Rio plays the noble peasant with a beautific expression, which is hard-ly character delineation, and Pedro Armendáriz, as her husband, lacks expression like a sphinx."[5]

Although American audiences did not appreciate Flor Silvestre, it established Del Rio as a top box office attraction in her native Mexico. Additionally, her portrayal of Esperanza was honored as the best performance by a screen actress in 1943. In her first Mexican film Dolores Del Rio earned an Ariel, the Mexican equivalent of the Oscar.

María Candelaria, released as Portrait Of Maria in the United States, reunited Del Rio with the success-ful team that created Flor Silvestre. Emilio Fernández returned as director, Gabriel Figueroa as cameraman, and Pedro Armendáriz as co-star. Maria Candelaria once again returns to the Mexican past of the pre-revolutionary era. In this period Mexican Indians are depicted as unfortunate victims of the ruling class.

As the film begins a newspaper reporter interviews a famous artist. The reporter is most interested in a por-trait of a nude woman which the painter refuses to sell.

The artist then explains the story of the remarkable
woman, María Candelaria. He recalls that he first met
María (Dolores Del Rio) in the Mexican city of Xochimilco
in 1909. María, the daughter of a prostitute, sells her
flowers in the market place. She is engaged to marry
Lorenzo Rafael (Pedro Armendáriz), a poverty-stricken
Indian laborer. Despite their love for each other, the
wedding seems destined never to take place. María becomes
ill from malaria, and is unable to afford a doctor or
medicine.

Lorenzo goes to the wealthy shopowner Damián, who
also loves María, and asks him for medicine. Damián is
jealous of Lorenzo, so he refuses, even though it might
cost María her life. Later that evening Lorenzo returns
to Damian's store to steal the quinine. While in the store,
Lorenzo also steals a wedding dress for María.

As the wedding ceremony begins, Damian arrives with
two policemen and they arrest Lorenzo. He is charged with
stealing quinine, a wedding dress, and a large sum of money.
Damián added the latter item to insure that Lorenzo would
be sent to jail. The judge sentences Lorenzo to a year
in prison despite his protestations of innocence.

María Candelaria turns to her only wealthy friend,
the artist, and asks him to post bail. He agrees, but he
cannot pay because the judge has left town for two weeks.
In the interim the painter persuades Maria to pose for him.
The artist decides to paint only her face, and then add
the nude body of another model.

Although the painter has graciously allowed Maria to
retain her modesty in his studio, he neglects to tell
others of his unusual arrangement. The townspeople believe
that María has posed in the nude, and they are shocked by
this breach in their moral code. Citizens burn Maria's
garden, and they stone her while she is waiting at the
jail. Lorenzo watches the murder, and escapes from his
guards in order to save María. Unfortunately, it is too
late, and María dies in his arms.

María Candelaria opened at the Cannes festival in a
late afternoon showing. Georges Sadoul recalled that the
auditorium was half empty, and, as the conversation between
the artist and the reporter began, members of the audience
began to leave. Then, almost as suddenly. the film turned

-63-

to the Mexican scenery and the faces of the Mexican people. The audience became interested, and many remained to see one of the most "fascinating films at the Cannes festival."

While Sadoul lauded the photography, direction, and script of <u>María Candelaria</u>, most of the praise went to Dolores Del Rio's performance: "We thought we knew her [Del Rio], but we have only seen her Hollywood face mask-- to use the language of the beauty parlor. Free of make- up, her face was surrounded by long braids. Dressed in the simple clothes of a Mexican peasant, Dolores Del Rio appeared completely new...Like her face, her acting was completely free of artifice. We did not have before us an actress, but a woman." As a result of the favorable notices, <u>Maria Candelaria</u> alerted film audiences to the advances in the Mexican and Latin American cinema.[6]

<u>Las Abandonadas</u> ("The Abandoned Ones") reunited the successful team of Del Rio, Armendáriz, Figueroa, and Fernández. Once again they returned to an analysis of Mexico's past in the revolutionary era. Margarita (Del Rio) has been abandoned by her husband Julio (Víctor Junco). When her father requests her to leave his home, she travels in search of her husband. She arrives in Mexico City and gives birth to a son named Margarito.

Margarita begins to work in a brothel. One evening General Juan Gómez (Armendáriz) arrives at the establish- ment. He spots the lovely Margarita and immediately falls in love with her. He buys her jewels and clothing, and installs her in an apartment in town. Margarita has never told Juan that she has a child from a previous marriage. When Juan finally proposes, she feels compelled to tell him the truth. He is not surprised by the news, since he has investigated Margarita and learned about her son. Indeed, Juan has already begun to send the child gifts. Margarita agrees to marry Juan and they go to the theater to celebrate.

As they leave the theater Juan is shot to death. Margarita learns that Juan was not the real General Gómez, but an imposter who had borrowed his uniform. The police arrest Margarita for complicity, and her son is sent to an orphanage. She must remain in jail for eight years.

Margarita returns from jail and searches for her son. She discovers that he has a brilliant future before him because of his talents as an orator. She is ashamed of her past, so she tells Margarito that his mother has died in prison.

Unable to find work, Margarita returns to the brothel. Yet, every month, she sends her son money. The son becomes a famous lawyer and he is praised by all. Margarita comes to the court house to hear her son speak. As he leaves the court room he notices a beggar woman and gives her a few pesos. The woman is Margarita, his mother. She says nothing as her son walks away. For her performance as Margarita, Dolores Del Rio won her second Ariel, one year after her first award.

Dolores Del Rio followed Las Abandonadas with Bugambilia. Released in 1945, Bugambilia represented another group effort of the Del Rio, Armendáriz, Figueroa, and Fernández team which was now at the forefront of the Mexican cinema. Like its predecessors, Bugambilia is a historical melodrama of nineteenth century Mexico.

In this film Dolores Del Rio portrays a member of the upper class. As Amalia, the daughter of a wealthy mine owner, she captivates the men of Guanajuato. She is loved by both Luis Felipe (Alberto Galán), a lawyer, and Ricardo (Armendáriz), a foreman at the mine. Amalia's father Don Fernando (Julio Villarreal) wishes his daughter to marry Luis Felipe, but she prefers Ricardo. Fernando sends Ricardo to the south so he will stay away from Amalia.

While working in the south of Mexico, Ricardo discovers a silver mine and becomes a wealthy man. He returns to Guanajuato and attempts to marry his beloved. As the young lovers leave for the church, Fernando discovers the plot. In a fit of anger he shoots Ricardo.

Luis Felipe defends Fernando on the charge of murder. In order to save her father, Amalia must claim that Ricardo tried to shoot Fernando. She lies in court, but it is to no avail. Her father cannot bear the guilt, and he shoots himself during the trial. Amalia then decides to live alone with the memory of Ricardo, rather than marry Luis Felipe.

Mexico's most successful production team separated after Bugambilia. Each member tackled new projects, and each received considerable praise for the new ventures.

Fernández wrote and directed <u>Pepita Jiménez</u> in 1945,
and Figueroa began work on <u>Cantaclaro</u>. Pedro Armendáriz
continued his string of brilliant acting performances.
He also appeared in <u>La Perla</u> ("The Pearl"), based on the
John Steinbeck story, in 1945, and shortly thereafter in
American films such as <u>The Fugitive</u> (1947) and <u>Three God-
fathers</u> (1948), both directed by John Ford.

By this date, Dolores Del Rio had become one of
Mexico's top box office attractions. She received fifty
thousand pesos for each film appearance as well as fifteen
per cent of the gross. Her first solo effort, <u>La Selva
de Fuego</u> ("The Jungle Of Fire") in 1945, did not receive
the critical acclaim of her earlier films. It lacked the
feeling for the Mexican landscape and personality that
Fernández had brought to her other Mexican films. As a
result, it seemed to parody standard Hollywood melodramas.
Yet, the film had one redeeming feature. It paired Del
Rio with Arturo de Córdoba, one of Mexico's leading dramatic actors, who had also performed in several American
films.

<u>La Otra</u> ("The Other"), released in 1946, was far
more successful. Dolores Del Rio displayed her talents
in a dual role. She portrayed both the wife of a million-
aire as well as her twin sister, a manicurist. Bette
Davis later remade the film in Hollywood as <u>Dead Ringer</u>
for Warner Brothers in 1964.

Magdalena (Del Rio) is widowed by the wealthy Montes
de Oca as the film opens. As Magdalena laments the loss
of her husband, her twin sister María laments the poverty
of her life in a seedy cafe. She visits her sister and
suddenly murders her. María changes clothes with her
sister and arranges the room so the murder will appear a
suicide. The victim, of course, will be the poor sister
María.

María poses as Magdalena and manages to fool almost
everyone. Even Fernando, Magdalena's former lover,
returns to the scene. María is forced to make love with
him lest he discover the plot.

Fernando begins to dominate Magdalena/María. He
demands large sums of money, and even appropriates several
of her classic paintings. Maria's former boyfriend, a
police agent, investigates Fernando's unusual behavior.
He discovers that Fernando and Magdalena had killed Montes

de Oca in an attempt to get his money. Maria is sentenced
to thirty years in prison for her sister's crime. She
was able to enjoy only one year of her sister's wealth.

La Otra began another lengthy association with a
single director for Dolores Del Rio. Roberto Gavaldón
directed four films for the Mexican actress. Yet, before
working with Gavaldón again, Del Rio began two foreign
projects. In 1947, she began John Ford's The Fugitive,
which is discussed in the next chapter. After completing
that film, she began a Latin American theater tour.
While in Argentina, she completed a film version of Oscar
Wilde's Lady Windermere's Fan entitled Historia de Una
Mala Mujer ("Story of an Evil Woman") for Spanish-speaking
audiences.

Del Rio returned to Mexico City in 1949, and began
work on La Malquerida ("The Hated One"), based on a play
by the Nobel Prize winning Spanish author Jacinto Bena-
vente. After a four year absence, the film reunited
Fernández, Figueroa, and Armendáriz once again.

Raimunda (Del Rio) marries the wealthy Esteban del
Soto (Armendáriz) after her first husband dies. Esteban
appears a kind and honest man, but his step-daughter Acacia
(Columba Domínguez) despises him since he has usurped the
position of her dead father. In order to escape from the
household, Acacia decides to marry Faustino, even though
she does not love him.

Faustino's family opposes the wedding. Rumor has it
that a previous suitor refused to marry Acacia since he
heard the saying, "He who loves a del Soto will have trouble
all his life." Nevertheless, Faustino and his father
Eusebio visit Esteban to ask the hand of his daughter.
Esteban refuses, and he virtually throws Faustino's family
out of the house. The reason for Esteban's stubborn attitude is finally revealed. He is in love with his step-
daughter.

One evening Faustino attempts to see Acacia, but
Esteban discovers him and shoots him. Esteban leaves
Faustino wounded on the floor. El Rubio, Esteban's servant,
has witnessed the event. He then kills the wounded Faustino.
Acacia testifies that her father was elsewhere on the night
of the murder and the court absolves him of guilt. Yet
Acacia overhears the true story of Faustino's death, and,

as a result, she becomes attracted to her step-father.
Esteban can no longer bear the guilt of his actions. He
asks his wife for forgiveness and then flees from the
family home. As he leaves he is discovered by the
Faustino family and killed for revenge. Acacia, now alone,
enters a convent as the film ends.

La Casa Chica ("The Small House"), directed by Roberto
Gavaldón, presents Dolores Del Rio in a contemporary drama
of unrequited love. Amalia (Del Rio), a medical student,
meets her classmate Fernando (Roberto Canedo) in the town
of San Esteban. Both are attempting to cure a plague which
is decimating the Chamula Indians. As they work together,
they soon fall in love. Amalia breaks her engagement to
Carlos, and Fernando decides to return to Mexico City to
break his engagement to Lucila Del Castillo.

While Carlos accepts the disappointing news graciously, Lucila is irate. She pretends to commit suicide.
Señor Del Castillo summons Fernando to his daughter's
deathbed. He suggests that Fernando fulfill his daughter's
last wish and marry her before she dies. They marry, and
Lucila suddenly "recovers." Fernando is trapped, and
Amalia, in desperation, continues her medical studies.

Years later Fernando and Amalia meet at a medical
conference. Both have become illustrious physicians.
They renew their acquaintance, and soon become lovers.
Fernando attempts to divorce Lucilla, but she refuses
to surrender custody of her son. As a result, Fernando
remains with his scheming wife since he loves his child
so much.

Amalia decides to return to Carlos, her childhood
sweetheart. Fernando hears word of the impending wedding,
and interrupts the ceremony. Amalia drops Carlos, and
once again becomes Fernando's lover.

Fernando's family becomes hostile to Amalia. His
son refuses to speak to her. When Fernando becomes ill,
no one will allow Amalia to see him. As Ferando dies,
he spots Amalia watching him from outside the window.
Lucila notices and shuts the window. She is alone as
her beloved dies.

Deseada ("The Desired One"), based on a play by
Margarita Xirgu, presented a melodrama of self-sacrifice

-68-

set amidst the Mayan ruins of the Yucatan. Both Dolores
Del Rio and her sister fall in love with the same man. The
gentleman in question prefers Dolores, but she cannot bear
to hurt her sister. Instead, Del Rio follows an ancient
Mayan ritual. She throws herself in the "well of the love-
lorn maidens" so her sister can wed the man of her dreams.

Doña Perfecta won Dolores Del Rio her third Ariel
in 1950. Based on the novel by Benito Pérez Galdos, this
film returned Del Rio to the historical dramas which had
been her mainstay since her Mexican debut in Flor Silvestre.
The Spanish locale of the novel was transferred to Mexico
of the late nineteenth century, and, as a result, the political context was fuzzy at best. Yet, the role of Doña
Perfecta, matriarch of a Conservative Mexican family,
allowed Dolores Del Rio to portray one of her richest and
most colorful roles.

Pepe Rey (Carlos Navarro) leaves Mexico City to visit
his aunt, Doña Perfecta (Del Rio), his cousin Rosario,
and his uncle Don Cayetano. He decides to remain with
his relatives while he is completing an engineering survey
for the central government. Pepe Rey is quite surprised
by his family. He immediately falls in love with his
cousin, Rosario (Esther Fernández), but is wary of his
aunt Doña Perfecta. From the moment Pepe meets his aunt
he is impressed by her domineering personality and her
old-fashioned habits.

Perfecta is disturbed by her young nephew who holds
the beliefs of modern science. She discovers "liberal"
books in his luggage and immediately has them burned
before the progressive ideals can contaminate her household. Furthermore, she refuses to allow her daughter
to consort with the young man from the city. In order that
Pepe will leave Santa Fe, Perfecta asks her influential
friends to have him removed from the government post.

Pepe mysteriously loses his job, but he refuses to leave
Santa Fe. Instead, he and Rosario decide to wed immediately. Perfecta cannot tolerate this insubordination,
so she locks Rosario in her room and tells Pepe that she
is ill. Perfecta also attempts to convince her daughter
that Pepe is an atheist and a believer in free love,
but she refuses to believe her mother's assertions.

As Liberal and Conservative armies clash in the
streets of Santa Fe, Pepe manages to find the key to

Rosario's room. As the lovers prepare to flee, Perfecta discovers the plot. She orders her servant to shoot Pepe in order to save her daughter from life with an atheist. Rosario sees Pepe shot, and she embraces her lover as he dies. She shouts that she despises her mother, and then she follows the soldiers who carry off Pepe's body. Perfecta can do nothing but pray before a statue of Christ as her house is destroyed by Liberal troops.

Reportaje ("Newspaper Reporting"), produced in 1953, featured virtually all of Mexico's top actors and actresses. Arturo de Cordova, María Félix, Pedro Armendáriz, and countless others joined with Dolores Del Rio in this Emilio Fernández film. Proceeds from the production were donated to ANDA (Asociación Nacional de Actores), Mexico's Actors' Fund. All of the performers contributed their services to the enterprise without pay.

Reportaje featured a series of short skits tied together by a newspaper reporter. Dolores Del Rio appeared with Arturo de Córdova in her scene, a tale of wealthy lovers.

Del Rio's work on Reportaje was completed quickly, and she appeared in El Niño y La Niebla ("The Child and the Madness") during the same year, 1953. Her performance as Marta won Del Rio her fourth Ariel for best performance by an actress.

Guillermo (Pedro López Lagar), a petroleum engineer, has noticed that his wife has acted strangely since the birth of their child Daniel. Yet, he is unable to explain Marta's unusual behavior.

Marta leaves for Mexico City to explain her problems to a doctor. It becomes apparent that mental illness has plagued Marta's family. Marta's mother has gone mad, and her brother has committed suicide. She is fearful of giving the madness to her children, so she conceals her family history from her first love Mauricio (Eduardo Noriega). Yet, when Marta explains that she does not wish to have any children, Mauricio leaves her.

Marta's mother becomes madder by the day. After she tries to set fire to the family home, Marta confines her to an insane asylum. In despair, Marta decides to marry Guillermo. Although she tries not to have children, young

Daniel (Alejandro Ciangherotti, Jr.) is born. Soon Marta begins to discover signs of madness in her son. She notices that he fears the dark, he is fascinated by fire, and he tends to sleepwalk. Unfortunately, these are the same signs of madness that first appeared in Marta's mother.

Years later Mauricio comes to the town where Marta and Guillermo live. He has been sent by the government to investigate a new drill bit that Guillermo has invented. Mauricio meets Marta, and she declares her love for him. She asks Guillermo for a divorce but he refuses. Marta then decides to take advantage of her son's trancelike state. Marta Gives Daniel a gun while he is sleepwalking, and she tell him to murder his father. As the child approaches Guillermo he suddenly wakes up and realizes what he is about to do. He is so stunned by this vile act that he shoots himself.

Marta confesses the truth to Guillermo and Mauricio, and her husband vows to remain by her side. Yet, the events have driven Marta to madness. As the film ends she waits for Daniel to return.

In 1954 Dolores Del Rio made her first film appearance in Spain. Señora Ama, a Mexican-Spanish co-production, featured Del Rio as a wealthy but unhappy woman of the Castilian countryside.

Although Feliciano (José Suárez) and his wife Dominica (Del Rio) own many farms and ranches, their marriage is unhappy. Dominica is unable to bear children, so Feliciano searches for greener pastures. He sires several illegitimate children, and Dominica agrees to raise them. Feliciano cannot control his urges, so he courts his wife's sister María Juana (María Luz Galicia). José, Feliciano's brother is also in love with the lovely María Juana.

It would be tempting to call this a love triangle, but it appears a rectangle. Aniceto, father of the two women, decides that this tomfoolery should not continue, and he urges Maria to marry José. Yet, even at the wedding, Feliciano's love for María becomes apparent.

Angered by this episode, Dominica retreats to the family estate at Umbría. Feliciano misses his wife, and he visits her and their love is renewed. Yet, all is not

well, as María Juana and José come to visit. José believes
that he sees Feliciano enter Maria's bedroom. He grabs a
gun and shoots the shrouded figure. Yet, the intruder is
merely Dominica visiting her sister. She is badly wounded
and collapses. As Feliciano rushes to her side she explains
that at last she is pregnant.

After Señora Ama was completed, Dolores Del Rio returned to Mexico to appear in A Donde Van Nuestros Hijos
("Where Are Our Children Going?") in 1956. Based on a
drama by Rodolfo Usigli entitled Medio Tono, this film
presented the problems of a modern Mexican family.

Martin (Tito Junco) and Rosa (Del Rio) have five
troublesome children. Julio is a Communist. Gabriela
loves a poor journalist named Eduardo, but has lived with
Carlos, a wealthy young man. Sara loves Alejandro, a
university student, even though her father disapproves.
Victor works in a luxury hotel and courts rich American
tourists. Martincito completes the list, since the new-
est child, David, dies at birth. The script would seem
to provide enough melodrama for several films.

Martin is unable to adapt to the new ways of his
children. He expects his children to obey his wishes
without question, but such expectations are old-fashioned.
Gabriela and Sara work in a store. Sara has an illegitimate child, but refuses to marry Alejandro. Julio is
arrested in a student demonstration. A wealthy super-
market owner tries to woo Rosa. As a result, Martin's life
seems to crumble. He finally decides that he and Rosa
should separate. As Martin and Rosa move the furniture
from their apartment they decide to reconcile their differences. The children settle their problems, and Martin
and Rosa take Martincito to another apartment where,
hopefully, they will live in peace and quiet.

La Cucaracha ("The Cockroach"), released in 1958, was
one of the few Dolores Del Rio Mexican films to open in the
United States. Starring María Félix, Emilio Fernández,
and Dolores Del Rio, La Cucaracha reminded American audiences
that Mexican film-makers were capable of excellent work.

A badly faded print opened at the Tivoli Theatre in
New York City, and the Times suggested that audiences see it:
"While the picture never rises in stature above its melodramatic plane and romantic embellishments, it is well
acted, crisply directed by producer Ismael Rodríguez, and

graphically photographed by Gabriel Figueroa...Señor
Rodríguez, through Señor Figueroa's camera, has created
a crackling fray that looks like the Fourth of July in an
Orozco art gallery."

Howard Thompson concluded his review with high praise
for the performers: "Both Señorita Felix, as the amoral
spitfire, and Señorita Del Rio, as her aristocratic ad-
versary, are persuasively passionate. Señor Fernández,
as their manly quarry, is excellent. Even minus real
depth, there is much to be said for a melodramatic eye-
filler as tough and tangy as this one. Neighbors below,
let's have more."[7]

Since Dolores Del Rio had left Hollywood, she had
appeared in sixteen Spanish language films within fifteen
years. During this period Hollywood producers had repeatedly beckoned Miss Del Rio to return to American films.
Yet, for a variety of reasons, Del Rio was unable to return to Hollywood. Finally John Ford, who had directed
Del Rio in The Fugitive in Mexico in 1947, asked the foremost Mexican star to appear in his new film, Cheyenne
Autumn. Del Rio approved of the project and thus she
embarked on the third stage of her motion picture career.
She was soon to become an international film star.

RETURN TO HOLLYWOOD

    After several years of acclaim in her native
Mexico, Dolores Del Rio began to welcome offers from
Hollywood, scene of her former triumphs. RKO offered
her an opportunity to work with the eminent American
director John Ford in a film version of Graham Greene's
novel <u>The Power And The Glory</u>. Perhaps the most
fortuitous circumstance of this production involved the
fact that Dolores Del Rio could remain in Mexico and
work with the foremost talents of the Mexican film
industry in this new motion picture.

    John Ford's <u>The Fugitive</u> (1947) was one of the
first Mexican-American co-productions. Ford entered
Mexico in 1946 with no equipment but a script, six
actors, including Henry Fonda and Dolores Del Rio, a
production manager, and two assistants. He relied on
Mexico's new Churubusco studios, partially owned by
Howard Hughes and RKO, for camera men, sound equipment
and technicians, extras, props, wardrobe, interpreters,
commissary, sets, and film laboratories.

    Ford's dependence on the Mexican film industry was
considered novel. Whenever Hollywood had previously
ventured over the border, the film companies brought
everything they needed with them. Henry King's <u>Captain
from Castile</u> company had arrived only shortly before
Ford, but what a difference! The Fox crew included a
full cast and production crew, eight freight loads of
equipment, plus cooks and commissary and a refrigerator

unit for preserving Technicolor film until it could be shipped to Hollywood for processing. King planned to shoot eight per cent of the film in Mexico, while Ford desired to complete the entire film in Mexico, either in the studio or on location.

Ford was pleasantly surprised with his Mexican crew members. Evidently the Hollywood denizens had expected real-life counterparts of the lazy Mexicans they had depicted on the screen, and the bustling efficiency of the Churbusco technicians surpassed all expectations. The North Americans were also startled by the modern equipment, the ample production facilities, and the sense of cooperation the Mexican workers displayed. Unlike Hollywood, Mexican film crews were organized in an industrial union. Hence, electricians could help carpenters, who in turn could help set designers, without the crossing of jurisdictional lines. North of the border, the craft unions dictated that the electrician could only work at his own skill. The rationale for this scheme in Mexico was quite deliberate. The fledgling film industry lacked Hollywood's skilled technicians. With no barriers among the various skills needed to produce the finished film product, a worker might learn various tasks until he discovers the one for which he is best suited. For this reason, Ford's relations with his Mexican crew were surprisingly satisfying.

Yet, Churubusco was not yet Hollywood, as minor technical problems plagued the brand new studio. For example, the bank of lights in the main building was anchored to the ceiling without any provision for lowering it. As a result, smaller sets had to be separately lit.

The crews also lacked the technical expertise of their Hollywood brethren. One scene called for a church in the town's central plaza. Ford noted that "in Hollywood, this church would have been half-inch plaster and the cobblestones would have been composition." The Mexican solution was to reproduce the church in all its splendor, with four walls of sides of foot-thick adobe. Even the street was laid with real cobblestones cemented in mortar. While this setting no doubt lent an air of reality to the proceedings, it was not easily removed after the shooting was finished. The church and the street had to be demolished with sledge-hammers, a time consuming process!

Ford's main problem in the initial days of filming was his lack of knowledge of the Spanish language. He was dependent on Emilio Fernández, one of Mexico's top directors at this time. Ford would explain his instructions softly to Fernández, who in turn would issue them in boisterous Spanish at the top of his lungs with extensive gestures and countless additions to the original instructions. Shortly thereafter, Ford began to notice that the actors and crew were beginning to call Fernández jefe ("chief"). As soon as Ford discovered the meaning of the word, he resolved to reassert his authority. One morning after Fernández had reinterpreted Ford's instructions and ordered technicians, actors, and extras into place, he shouted, "Silencio!", and then waited for Ford to whisper "Roll 'em." Ford hesitated for several lengthy minutes until his crew realized that Fernández was ultimately dependent on Ford for his final instructions. With this message clearly understood, Ford whispered, "Roll 'em." From then on the American director was known as the jefe.[1]

The Fugitive is curious in its ideology from a Mexican viewpoint. Although the film glorifies a Mexican priest (Henry Fonda), it reveals a black picture of Mexican politics and society. After the Mexican Revolution, the Constitution of 1917 limited the excessive powers the Church had acquired from Spain during the colonial period. The new charter affirmed freedom of religion, nationalized clerical property, made marriage a civil contract, and prohibited clerical participation in politics. Although the Constitution thus dictated the legal separation of Church and State, and the ultimate secularization of Mexican society, the majority of these new laws were not enforced in the hectic period following the revolution. However, in 1926 the regime of Plutarco Elías Calles began the implementation of these laws, and prohibited alien priests, closed religious schools, and ordered priests to register with State authorities so their political activity might be regulated. In response, the clergy went on a three-year strike, closing the churches and refusing to administer Catholic rituals. Large sectors of the peasantry supported the priests, and guerilla activity against the government was frequent in this violent period of Mexican history.[2] Ford's film ignores the historical complications, and concentrates only on the role of one priest as a victim in a corrupt society bent on the elimination of all religion.

The story is timeless and biblical in form. From the moment the priest opens the door of the parish church and his shadow falls on the floor in the shape of a cross, the religious dimension of the film is apparent. Fonda is a fugitive Mexican priest. He returns to his former church, now closed, and wishes to baptize the children of the village who had been denied the sacrament. As the priest enters the church, he is surprised by a Mexican woman, Maria Dolores (Dolores Del Rio), who is hiding in the shadows. Maria is startled at first. She believes the intruder is from the secret police and will arrest her for attending church. The priest explains his mission and Maria kisses his hand. She explains that she has an unbaptized child but no husband. She wishes the priest to baptize her daughter "so when she gets married, she can be called by name."

The priest agrees to baptize the child and he urges Maria to summon the other villagers to the celebration. Maria explains that the women will not follow her since she has an illegitimate child. In anger, the priest rings the church bells in defiance of the authorities. The townspeople bring their children to the church, and Maria's daughter is the first to be baptized.

Meanwhile, in a nearby town, the Police Lieutenant (Pedro Armendáriz) arrives as the Police Chief (Leo Carrillo) is sentencing those recently arrested. The criminals, gamblers, and drunks receive five peso fines, while a man accused of owning a holy medal is sentenced to two months in jail. The Lieutenant cannot understand why the prisoner has a holy medal, since "the last priest was shot six months ago." The Chief hates to disillusion his subordinate, but he admits that "there is still another priest left." The problem, according to the Lieutenant, is that "the superstitious villagers hide the priest." He decides to gather hostages from every village and shoot them unless the villagers deliver the priest.

The Lieutenant arrives at the town where the fugitive is hiding. As his troops terrorize the village, he decides to search the church. As he enters he discovers Maria Dolores and her baby. They have met before and it soon becomes clear that the Lieutenant is the missing father. He is shocked to find Maria in this village:

      Lieutenant: What are you doing here? Why did
                           you leave your village?

Maria Dolores:	My father made me leave after you left!
Lieutenant:	I meant to come back. But I had work to do. We're making a better world, Maria Dolores. (He points to the child.) For him, too.
Maria Dolores:	It's a girl--like me.
Lieutenant:	How do you make a living? Do you work?
Maria Dolores:	I work--(She shows him the rose in her hair) in a canteen.

Before he can reply to this shocking revelation, a second policeman arrives and chases Maria from the church. As she leaves, she pauses and crosses herself.

The fugitive realizes that he can no longer endanger the villagers by his presence. He tells Maria of his intentions and he leaves the same evening. He arrives at the coast and is waiting to board a ship to the United States, when a young boy recognizes him. He explains that his grandfather is dying and he needs a priest to administer the last rites. The priest agrees to follow the youth.

The boy's relatives explain that wine is needed for the ritual. Since the sale of alcoholic beverages is prohibited, they direct the priest to an illicit dealer. As the priest leaves the salesman, the Chief of Police enters. He and the dealer drink most of the priest's wine, but he is able to escape before they recognize him. Yet, moments later, another policeman discovers the priest with a half empty bottle of wine. As a result, he is tossed in jail for drunkeness.

A few days later the fugitive once again attempts to leave the country. He goes to Maria Dolores' canteen and asks for help. Although he is tired, Maria insists that they begin the journey in the darkness. As she prepares to leave, the priest falls asleep. Maria covers him with a blanket. Shortly thereafter, the police arrive. They were informed that the priest was hiding in the canteen. Maria flirts with the men and gives them free alcohol. She even decides to dance for the police. As she changes her clothing, she warns the priest to flee and wait for her across the river.

She swiftly returns to dance for the police and
hopefully distract them from their mission. As she is
performing for the troops, the Police Lieutenant arrives.
He throws her to the floor, and commands his men to
continue their search.

As the priest flees from the police, he meets El
Gringo (Ward Bond), a criminal. As the police arrive,
El Gringo assumes they are pursuing him and he opens fire.
The confusion allows the priest to escape to a neighboring
state which is sympathetic to the clerical cause. The
former fugitive enters a sanatorium in an attempt to
regain his health.

Several months later a police informer (J. Carrol
Naish) arrives at the villa. He tells the priest that
El Gringo has been wounded during a bank robbery and he
needs a priest to administer the last rites. Despite the
danger, the priest resolves to return and help the man who
had helped him escape. As he arrives at the hut where
the wounded criminal is waiting, he is greeted by the
Police Lieutenant and his men. It is a trap.

The Lieutenant offers the priest a chance to live
if he renounces his religion, but he refuses. The
Lieutenant feels guilty about the priest's fate when he
discovers that he baptized his illegitimate child. As
the shot is heard, the Lieutenant grabs his heart as
though he himself had been executed.

The film ends on a note of hope. A new priest
returns to the village. As he enters the church, he is
bathed in light. He walks forward, and a shadow of the
cross, from the grating on the door, fills the screen.
The Catholic religion has survived.

After Dolores Del Rio completed The Fugitive, she
returned to her new career in Mexican films. In 1954,
Hollywood beckoned once again, as Twentieth-Century-Fox
offered her a role in Broken Lance. Negotiations proceed-
ed quickly, and Miss Del Rio prepared for her return to
the United States by applying for a visa from the American Embassy on February 18. By March 2, it was referred
to Washington under the McCarran-Walter Immigration Act,
which required screening of all visitors and immigrants
to the United States. Perhaps Dolores Del Rio's investigation for Communist activities in 1934 had slowed the
entry process. In the McCarthy era such an occurrence
would hardly have been surprising. After this revelation

Del Rio fled to a friend's house in Cuernavaca and remained in seclusion during this controversy. Her producer, Francisco Cabrera, was irate. He noted that "there are over twenty American film stars working here now. Why should we let them come here when they insult Mexico's first actress?"[3]

Twentieth-Century-Fox waited only a few more days and announced that they could wait no longer for the Mexican actress since filming had already begun. They replaced Del Rio with Katy Jurado, who had performed in <u>High</u> <u>Noon</u>. Her triumphant return to the Hollywood screen was thus swiftly aborted.[4]

Although motion pictures did not page Dolores Del Rio for another screen role until 1960, television sought her dramatic talents. She returned to Hollywood in 1957 to appear on the <u>Schlitz</u> <u>Playhouse</u> <u>of</u> <u>Stars</u> in an episode entitled "An Old Spanish Custom." She received no trouble from immigration officials at this later date. CBS called her again to perform in "The Public Prosecutor", a drama by Theodore Apstein for the <u>United</u> <u>States</u> <u>Steel</u> Hour. She portrayed a clever French woman who tricks a sinister public prosecutor (Walter Slezak) into signing his own death warrant during the bloody days of the French Revolution.

Prior to this performance, she appeared at an interview which stunned those present. The great Mexican actress had apparently remained ageless. She commented to the assembled crowd, "I keep busy, keep interested and keep loving things, people and nature. When you become bored, then you grow old." The critic for the <u>New</u> <u>York</u> <u>Times</u> also was entranced by Miss Del Rio: "As she spoke during lunch in a hotel dining room, Miss Del Rio was attracting admiring glances from other guests nearby. Their interest was understandable. The star's appearance had undergone no marked change since her days of Hollywood stardom. Her brown eyes flashed as she talked enthusiastically about her work. She was wearing a turquoise gown created by the Paris couturier, Balenciaga. Complementing it were a turquoise ring, necklace and earrings. Waiters and busboys lingered as they attended her."

In her interview, Miss Del Rio gave most of her words of praise to television: "I think it's quite wonderful how the horizons of acting have enlarged. There are now three major mediums of entertainment, all having

their own advantages and disadvantages. Motion picture
actresses many years ago were just motion picture
actresses. But you learn a great deal by making the ad-
justments that you have to make by working in television,
the motion pictures and on the stage."[5]

The reference to the stage also marked a new
direction for Dolores Del Rio's talents. Prior to her
television performance, she had appeared in American
summer stock performances of Anastasia. As soon as she
finished "The Public Prosecutor", she returned to Mexico
City for rehearsals of Oscar Wilde's Lady Windermere's
Fan. In 1959, she married Lewis A. Riley, Jr., a
theater producer in Latin American countries, who en-
couraged her to appear in his Argentine production of
Robert E. Sherwood's The Road To Rome.[6] Thus, although
Dolores Del Rio had not appeared in a motion picture in
Hollywood since Journey Into Fear in 1943, she was hardly at rest during the interim.

Dolores Del Rio returned to the United States to
appear as Elvis Presley's mother in Flaming Star (1960).
After her screen triumphs of earlier years, this may have
hardly seemed an auspicious role. Yet, the strong screenplay by Nunnally Johnson and Clair Huffaker and the capable direction of Don Siegal provide a sentimental and
emotional vehicle for Dolores Del Rio's return to Hollywood.[7]

The film considers a topic that had been discussed
in earlier Del Rio films. Elvis Presley portrays Pacer,
the halfbreed, caught between the white world of his
father (John McIntire) and the Indian culture of his
mother (Del Rio). Neither the white settlers nor the
Indian tribesmen are willing to accept this product of a
mixed marriage. He is suspected by all, and trusted by
no one.

Although earlier films had considered the plight of
the halfbreed, Flaming Star views Pacer with a new found
sympathy. While the mixed-blood of the silent era had
been habitually portrayed as a villain, Pacer becomes an
heroic figure, faithful to his beleaguered family at whatever the cost. No doubt the casting of Elvis Presley in
the role of Pacer helped to determine the sympathetic
nature of the character. Nevertheless, by 1960 Hollywood
westerns were beginning to recognize that Indians were not

really the barbarous savages that had been presented
in motion pictures. The screen writers valiantly
attempt to consider the conquest of the west from the
Indian point of view. Once this is understood, the
sterotype of the bloodthirsty savage is all but eliminated in the film. It is for this reason that Flaming
Star should be remembered.

Two cowboys approach a farmhouse late one night.
It is dark, and the cowhands become suspicious. As they
cautiously enter the room, the Burton family jumps from
the shadows and sings "Happy Birthday." The expected
ambush becomes a surprise party. All the neighbors join
in the party for Clint (Steve Forrest). They bring gifts,
and compliment Neddy Burton (Del Rio) on her delicious
cooking.

Yet, the happy atmosphere will soon vanish. As the
neighbors return home they are greeted by an Indian war
party. The Kiowas kill, steal the horses, and set the
house on fire. Only one neighbor, Will Howard, with an
arrow lodged in his shoulder, manages to escape from the
Indians by hiding in a storm cellar.

The Burton family hears of the massacre, and they,
too, notice that Kiowa Indians are watching their farm
from afar. Buffalo Horn (Rudolph Acosta) approaches the
house and wishes to speak to Pacer. Pacer refuses since
he fears an ambush in the darkness. He tells Buffalo
Horn to return when it is light. Neddy scoffs at her
son's fears: "They wouldn't do anything to us." Nevertheless, Pa reminds her that some Indians still call her
"the thin woman who deserted her own people," and cautions
her to be on her guard.

Pa, Clint, and Pacer ride to the nearest Wells Fargo
office in search of weapons. Angus Pierce (Richard Jaeckel)
greets his friends from the party of the previous night with
a gun. All are welcome but Pacer, since Angus believes he
is in cahoots with the Indians. The sense of friendship
begins to dissolve as the neighboring families feel that
the Burton house is safe from Indian attack since Neddy is
of Kiowa origin. The blissful world of the Burtons slowly
begins to dissolve as the neighbors decide they can no
longer be trusted.

The next day a group of local farmers ride to the
Burton house with weapons drawn. "Are you with us or

against us?" asks one. Pa is amazed that his friends
of twenty years can ask such a question. Another shouts,
"With all the half-breeds in the family this question
must be asked!" A third rancher insults Neddy. Clint
becomes enraged and shoots him. Neddy, an accomplished
nurse, attempts to bandage the wounds, but the rancher
rejects her aid. ("Who wants help from a dirty Indian!")
The farmers leave, and stampede the Burton's cattle as
they go. Pacer is disillusioned by the turn of events:
"These are what we call our white friends, I suppose."

Pa and Clint leave shortly after to search for
their cattle. Pacer is left to protect Neddy. Hours
later, two strangers approach the farm. They are
hungry trappers in need of a meal. Despite Pacer's
warnings, Neddy insists that they be fed. As the trappers
enter, they discover that Neddy is an Indian and Pacer
is a half-breed. They call Pacer "Red-Boy" and one
attempts to kiss Neddy. ("Where's your husband? You like
'em white, huh? I like you red babies.") Pacer returns
with a rifle and, rather than shoot the trappers, he
fights them until they beg for mercy. As Pacer returns
to the farmhouse, the trappers flee into the mountains.

The next morning Buffalo Horn returns to the farm.
He wants Pacer to join his warriors, since a half-breed
who abandons white civilization will bring success to his
cause. If Pacer refuses, Buffalo Horn vows to burn the
Burton farm and murder all within. Pacer returns to
discuss the problem with his mother. Not to be threatened, Neddy decides to return to the Kiowa land to discuss
the problem with the leaders of the village.

Pacer and Neddy return with Buffalo Horn to the
Kiowa village. After long discussions, Buffalo Horn
realizes that Pacer is not ready to join the Kiowas.
Despite the fact that Pacer has been mistreated by whites,
Buffalo Horn senses that the youth still identifies with
white culture. He advises the youth to return to his
home and consider his dilemma. If in doubt, Buffalo Horn
tells Pacer to ask himself three questions:
1. Who owns this land?
2. Who has been here since the beginning of
time?
3. Do we steal the land of the farmers?
If Pacer can answer these questions in good faith, Buffalo
Horn is confident that he will join the Kiowa warriors.

As Pacer leaves, Buffalo Horn wishes him well.

Neddy's encounter with her Kiowa relatives is far
less successful. None of the elders would speak to her
since she had betrayed her tribe: "They said I wasn't
Kiowa--or white either." As she leaves the village, she
begins to cry. Meanwhile, a shot is heard and Neddy is
suddenly wounded. The murderer, Will Howard, had escaped the Indian attack on his ranch by hiding in the
cellar, and, still wounded, has been wandering in the
desert searching for revenge. Pacer kills him with a
single shot.

Neddy is mortally wounded. As Pacer arrives at
her side, she claims to hear "the flaming star of death."
As she lapses into unconsciousness, Pa and Clint arrive
and bring her to their ranch. Pa is extremely worried,
so he asks his sons to go to town and find Doc Phillips
(Ford Rainey). Once again, as the boys reach town, they
are greeted by men with rifles. They refuse to allow the
doctor to help the family of half-breeds. One shouts,
"Get a medicine man!"

Pacer refuses to let his mother die. He returns
to town and kidnaps Phillips' daughter. He will ex-
change one life for another. If Phillips comes to the
Burton farm, Pacer will release the girl. Naturally,
Phillips agrees.

As Pacer and Clint are trying to persuade the
doctor to help them, Neddy suddenly awakes. She clutches
her scarf, leaves the cabin, and begins to walk toward
the mountains in order to be with her ancestors. She
is unable to reach her goal. Pa finds her lying near the
outskirts of the farm. Once again, she claims to hear
"the flaming star of death." As Pa weeps, Neddy expires.

Neddy's death changes Pacer's life. He blames
the whites for his mother's fate ("All she was to them
was a squaw. White men shot her and white men let her
die...Those people down at thecrossing, I want to see
every one of them dead.") Pacer says good-bye to his
father, and explains that he is going to join the Kiowas.
He visits Buffalo Horn and tells him that he is returning
to his people. He asks only one favor, that he will
never have to fight his father or brother. Buffalo Horn
agrees and Pacer becomes a Kiowa.

As Pacer is inducted into the Kiowa tribe, a
roving hand of warriors kills Pa. Clint discovers the
arrow-ridden body of his father and is determined to
seek revenge. He attempts to shoot Buffalo Horn, but
he misses and the Indians pursue him. Clint is wounded
and he hides in the underbrush. Pacer realizes that
his true allegiance is to his brother, so he leads
the warriors away from Clint. Pacer returns and ties
the unconscious Clint to his horse. Fortunately, the
horse brings Clint to the Wells Fargo station where he
is helped by his girlfriend Roslyn (Barbara Eden).

Pacer arrives at the station the next morning. He
is badly wounded. Clint goes to help his brother, but
Pacer urges him to stay away: "Don't come any closer. I
just wanted to see if you were all right. Live for me
Clint. Maybe someday, somewhere people will understand
folks like us. When I was fighting the Kiowas, I saw
the flaming star of death." As Clint watches, Pacer
returns to the hills to die in the land of his ancestors.

Cheyenne Autumn (1964), like Flaming Star, attempts
to view the American Indian sympathetically. The James R.
Webb screen play, suggested by a book by Mari Sandoz, is
supposedly based on historical fact. In 1878 almost eight
hundred Cheyennes left their reservation in the Southwest
to return to the land of their ancestors near Yellowstone.
This fifteen hundred mile journey across the Great Plains
is the focus of Cheyenne Autumn.

On September 7, 1878, on the Cheyenne Reservation,
the Indians wait for the arrival of a Congressional Commit-
tee. Hopefully, the congressmen will grant permission for
the Cheyennes to return to their distant homeland. As
they wait, the Spanish Woman (Dolores Del Rio) sifts the
barren desert sands through her fingers and prays for a
return to the fertile land of her ancestors.

Captain Thomas Archer (Richard Widmark) had arranged
for the Congressional visit so "every bigwig in Washington
could see how the Cheyennes had been forgotten." Apparently
they are about to be forgotten once again. As the Indians
wait in the heat of the desert sun, the congressmen are no-
where to be seen. The eldest Indians begin to faint from
exhaustion. The Spanish Woman attempts to help the victims,
but Red Shirt (Sal Mineo), a headstrong young brave, forbids it.

The Indians learn that the officials will not arrive that day. Little Wolf (Ricardo Montalban) has lost all patience, and he stalks off. "Remember to obey the law," shouts Captain Archer. Little Wolf replies, "We are asked to remember much, but the white man remembers nothing." As he leaves, Little Wolf tells the Quaker missionaries, led by Deborah Wright (Carroll Baker), that the children will no longer attend school: "Our children must not learn the white man's lying words."

Archer is frustrated by Little Wolf's attitude. He tells Deborah that Cheyennes are "fierce, smart, and meaner than sin from the day they are born." She is unable to understand his attitude. "You only think of the past, and I think of the future."

The Spanish Woman tells Deborah that the Cheyennes are going to return to their tribal homeland. She is upset by this revelation and is extremely worried about the welfare of her Cheyenne friends. After considerable prayer, she decides to join the Cheyennes on their great trek. She will care for the children and educate them.

Archer discovers that the Indians and his beloved Deborah have disappeared, and the cavalry pursues them. Archer is disturbed by his assistant who is anxious to kill an Indian to revenge his father's death. Archer warns the young man as the troops leave: "The army's role is to keep peace. The Indians broke no law by leaving the reservation. Only if they cross the river is the law broken."

The Cheyennes discover that the white men are folowing them and they prepare for battle. Interestingly, unlike most Hollywood Indians, the Cheyennes converse in dialect. The audience understands the situation due to the presence of Deborah who continually asks the Spanish Woman for translations of the conversations.

The Cheyennes prepare to ambush the army troops, but Archer suspects their intent. Nevertheless, a trigger-happy officer starts the battle too hastily, and several soldiers are killed. The Indians bury their dead, and continue their journey homeward.

Newspapers print accounts of the "massacre", and the death toll mysteriously mounts in each succeeding headline. Action is demanded from Washington as the Indians continue to evade detection.

<u>Cheyenne</u> <u>Autumn</u> presents a jaundiced picture of the
Washington establishment. The government seems controlled by land speculators who argue that the Indians
stand in the way of progress. The only defender of the
Indians in the entire city is the head of the Department
of the Interior, Carl Schurz (Edward G. Robinson). He
calls the speculators and their Senators "dollar patriots",
since they treat the Indians like Negro slaves before the
Civil War. He berates the lobbyists: " Your only purpose
is to own every acre of land the Indians once thought they
owned." As the speculators see that Schurz is adamant,
they begin to scheme to remove the Bureau of Indian
Affairs from his control.

    As the Cheyennes continue their journey, food becomes
scarce and the land becomes barren. The once proud
Indians are now forced to beg for food. Hunger over-
rides their inherent caution, and several are killed as
they wander too close to settlements in search of food.
As the Indians travel, Deborah continues to teach the
young children. One day she draws a picture of a buffalo,
but none of the children can identify it since they have
never seen one. The next day the Cheyennes do discover
buffalo, but they arrive too late. White hunters have
already stripped the animals of their valuable hides and
allowed the flesh to rot. As winter arrives, the Cheyennes
are desperate.

    In the state of Nebraska, the Indians hold a con-
ference. Half resolve to continue the march, the others
decide to return to Fort Robinson. Deborah, starving and
in ill health, follows the latter group.

    Although these Cheyennes return voluntarily to the
reservation, they are not greeted warmly by the German
Captain Wessels (Karl Malden). He insists that the Indians
be kept under restraint, and that they be returned to
their original reservation in the deserts of the Southwest. Archer argues with his superior when he hears the
order: "But these people cannot survive this trek in the
dead of winter." Wessels replies, "I agree with you,
but an order is an order." Wessels locks the Indians in an
unheated warehouse. However, unbeknownst to the army
officers, the Cheyennes have guns and weapons hidden in
their clothing.

    Dull Knife (Gilbert Roland) threatens to kill him-
self when he hears of their forced return. The Spanish

Woman explains to Archer that others will follow: "They will not go back. Life there is not life. They will die here. They will die here." Archer finds the situation intolerable, and he resolves to go to Washington and inform Secretary Schurz of the events occurring at Fort Robinson:

> Schurz: I heard they were being--what's the word? - "restrained."
> Archer: The right word is "murder."

A telegram arrives at Fort Robinson which relieves Wessels from his command and he is confined to quarters. A kindly doctor attempts to free the Cheyennes from their prison, but the Indians murder their intended savior and flee from the army camp. Wessels hears the shooting and breaks out of his room. He sees the Indians gone and his guards dead. He stares blankly into space, a man driven to madness.

The freed Cheyennes rendezvous with Little Wolf at a victory cave in the Dakotas. They are spotted by the cavalry and surrounded. The weakened Indians are unable to fight and a massacre seems imminent. Suddenly Schurz and Archer arrive. Schurz demands to talk to the Cheyennes before the attack, but the cavalry commander refuses. Schurz cleverly pulls rank on the officer: "Do you enjoy killing Indians--men, women, and children? If you do not allow me to talk with them, I will consider you trespassers on government ground [and have you evicted!]."

Schurz speaks calmly to the Indians: "I know many promises have been made to you and have been broken. I am not going to make promises like these." He vows that he will tell the American people about Fort Robinson and allow the Cheyennes to return to their native land. Red Shirt (Sal Mineo) refuses to accept the white man's word. He reaches for his gun and is swiftly shot. The Spanish Woman grieves once more as yet another Cheyenne dies. The film ends on a hopeful note as the Chief accepts Schurz's guarantees and Deborah returns to the world of the white man, believing that the Cheyennes will at last be free.

Despite John Ford and James Well's sympathy with the Indian viewpoint in Cheyenne Autumn, the screenplay ignores several crucial facts. These distortions minimize

-89-

the suffering of the Cheyennes, and exalt the efforts
of the American government to ease their plight. First,
the film neglects to explain the reason the Cheyennes
are living in the middle of the desert. Actually, an
1868 treaty signed by Little Wolf and Dull Knife had
committed them to live either on the Sioux reservation
or on a reservation set apart for the Southern Cheyennes.
The army chose the latter option, and the Cheyennes
accepted with the understanding that they could return
to their native land if they found the new reservation
unsatisfactory. As the film suggests, the new homeland
was a disappointment. There was insufficient food and
water, and the desert heat and climate was unbearable.
Disease became rampant, and Little Wolf complained:
"Our people died, died, died, kept following one another
out of this world." When the Indians requested permission
to leave, as they believed their treaty allowed, it was
denied by the War Department.

     While the causes of the Indian exodus are slight-
ly obscured, the depiction of the new Secretary of the
Interior, Carl Schurz, is a gross distortion. Schurz
and Edward G. Robinson resembled each other only in looks.
The Indians called Schurz "Big Eyes", and they were
amazed that a man with such large eyes could know so
little. Schurz initially agreed with General Sheridan's
assessment that the Cheyennes must return to their reservation. ("Unless they are sent back to where they came
from, the whole reservation system will receive a shock
which will endanger its stability.") Schurz did not
assume the activist role that is presented in Cheyenne
Autumn. He was hardly a champion of the Cheyenne cause,
and when the tribe was eventually allowed to return to
its homeland after months of bureaucratic delay, only a
few of the original migrants remained alive.[8]

     Dolores Del Rio's last non-Spanish film, More Than
A Miracle (1967), a French and Italian co-production,
was released in the United States by Metro-Goldwyn-Mayer.
By all accounts, this Sophia Loren vehicle was an un-
mitigated disaster. The New York Times commented, "The
picture does have a certain social-historical interest,
neatly dramatizing the great technical strides Hollywood
has taken in the last 30 years without getting anywhere.
With the exception of Omar Sharif, who plays the prince,
and Dolores Del Rio and George Wilson, the picture seems
to have been made entirely by and with Italians, in Italy.

but its soul is in southern California." The review continued, calling the film a "mess" and a "disaster area."[9]

   More Than A Miracle is set in medieval Spain,
where the handsome Prince Ramon (Omar Sharif) must select
a bride from seven of the kingdom's most beautiful women.
The Princess Mother (Dolores Del Rio) becomes distressed
when her son refuses to accept any of her choices. Instead Ramon ignores his stately duties, and wanders into
the countryside. In a nearby monastery he meets a mysterious friar, Brother Joseph (Leslie French) who is
able to fly through the air, much to the delight of local
children. Brother Joseph resolves to help Ramon in his
quest for the perfect wife. He gives the Prince a donkey
and a bag of flour. The ideal woman will be the one who
makes him seven dumplings.

   As the Prince leaves the monastery, he meets a
lovely peasant woman named Isabella (Sophia Loren). He
instructs her to prepare seven dumplings, but, overcome
by hunger, Isabella eats the seventh dumpling. The
Prince scolds her for her disobedience and pretends that
he has died. Isabella seeks advice from a coven of witches,
who give her a magic spell to return the Prince to life.
Unfortunately, Isabella forgets the correct incantation,
and accidentally paralyzes her beloved Prince.

   Ramon's soldiers seek the peasant woman and bring
her to the castle. She breaks the spell of paralysis
with a kiss. Despite Ramon's affection for Isabella,
he feels she must be punished. He seals her in a barrel
and rolls it toward the sea. Fortunately, she is res-
cued by some urchins, and she manages to return to the
palace to work as a kitchen maid.

   The viceroy is becoming annoyed by Ramon's refusal
to select a bride. He orders the Prince to chose from
the seven princesses. Ramon, now in love with Isabella,
disguises her as a princess and enters her in a dish-
washing contest which will determine who will be his
bride. Isabella's dishes break as soon as she touches
them due to a clever trick on the part of a jealous rival.
Since she has lost her Prince, Isabella decides to drown
herself. Brother Joseph returns as a heavenly saint and
prevents the suicide. He returns Isabella to the castle
where she reveals the plot of her jealous rival. She is
now able to marry the Prince as the film ends.

At this date, <u>More</u> <u>Than</u> <u>A</u> <u>Miracle</u> remains Dolores
Del Rio's last non-Spanish language film. Despite this
fact, Dolores Del Rio can in no way be considered in
retirement. She has remained active in film, television,
and theater in her native Mexico and has devoted considerable time to a variety of charities.

Dolores Del Rio's return to Hollywood revealed
several important trends. Despite a new found sympathy
for the Mexican, and Native-American in the films of
this era, it is apparent that Dolores Del Rio might have
become typecast had she remained in Hollywood. In <u>The</u>
<u>Fugitive</u> she portrays a Mexican peasant, and in <u>Flaming</u>
<u>Star</u> and <u>Cheyenne</u> <u>Autumn</u> she is an Indian. This is a
far cry from the Del Rio films of the 1930's. At that
time, her nationality did not limit the scope of her
screen roles. Unfortunately, by the 1960's, she seemed
cast in a sterotyped role. Indeed, as her husband recently commented, "But would you believe? Dolores <u>still</u> gets
many offers to do squaws."10 Perhaps for this reason in
recent years, the center of her career has remained Mexico
and Latin America.

VII. AT PRESENT

It would be difficult to speak of retirement for
Dolores Del Rio. Although she has curtailed her film
appearances somewhat in recent years, she still performs
occasionally on the stage and television. Most of her
spare time is filled with charity work. She devotes
considerable effort to the creation of nursery schools.

At present, Del Rio is considered one of the most
famous stars Mexico has produced. Film retrospectives
of her work are frequent, and she is continually honored by both government officials and film stars.

A recent testimonial on April 23, 1976, celebrated
Del Rio's half century of contributions to the motion
picture art. A friend, García Borja, praised Dolores
Del Rio for her accomplishments: "Del Rio's career
has two sides. She has contemplated the glories of

Hollywood, but she has never forgotten the true nature of the Mexican people."[1] The fact that Dolores Del Rio returned to her homeland endeared her to her fellow citizens. For this reason, a standing ovation and cries of "Bravo" greeted her as she entered the theater.

APPENDIX

MOTION PICTURE PERFORMANCES

1.   JOANNA (First National Pictures, 1925)
     Production: Producer and Director: Edwin Carewe.
Script: Lois Leeson. Photography: Robert B. Kurrle
and A.M. Greene.
     Cast: Dorothy Mackaill (Joanna Manners), Jack
Mulhall (John Wilmore), Paul Nicholson (Frank Brandon),
George Fawcett (Anthony Eggleson), John T. Murray (Lord
Teddy Dorminster), Rita Carewe (Georgie Leach), Dolores
Del Rio (Carlotta de Silva), Lillian Langdon (Mrs.
Roxanna Adams), Edwards Davis (Grayson), Bob Hart (The
Chauffeur).

2.   HIGH STEPPERS (First National Pictures, 1926)
     Production: Producer and Director: Edwin Carewe.
Script: Lois Leeson. Photography: Robert Kurrle.
     Cast: Lloyd Hughes (Julian Perryam), Mary Astor
(Audrey Nye), Dolores Del Rio (Evelyn Iffield), Rita
Carewe (Janet Perryam), John T. Murray (Cyril Buckland),
Edwards Davis (Victor Buckland), Alec B. Francis (Father
Perryam), Clarissa Selwyn (Mrs. Perryam), Charles Sellon
(Grandpa Perryam), John Steppling (Major Iffield), Emily
Fitzroy (Mrs. Iffield), Margaret McWade (Mrs. Clancy).

3.   PALS FIRST (First National Pictures, 1926)
     Production: Producer and Director: Edwin Carewe.
Script: Lois Leeson. Photography: Robert B. Kurrle.
Titles: Ralph Spence.
     Cast: Lloyd Hughes (Richard Castleman/Danny Row-
land), Dolores Del Rio (Jeanne Lamont), Alec Francis
(Dominie), George Cooper (The Squirrel), Edward Earle
(Dr. Harry Chilton), Hamilton Morse (Judge Lamont),
George Reed (Uncle Alex), Alice Nichols (Aunt Caroline),
Alice Belcher (Charley Anderson).

4.   THE WHOLE TOWN'S TALKING (Universal-Jewel, 1926)
     Production: Producer: Carl Laemmle. Director:
Edward Laemmle. Script: Raymond Cannon. Photography:
Charles Stumar.
     Cast: Edward Everett Horton (Chester Binney), Vir-
ginia Lee Corbin (Ethel Simmons), Trixie Friganza (Mrs.
Simmons), Otis Harlan (Mr. Simmons), Robert Ober (Donald
Mont-Allen), Aileen Manning (Mrs. Van Loon), Hayden
Stevenson (Tom Murphy), Margaret Quimby (Sadie Wise),
Dolores Del Rio (Rita Renault), Malcolm Waite (Jack
Shields).

5. WHAT PRICE GLORY (Fox Film Corporation, 1926)
Production: Producer: William Fox. Director:
Raoul Walsh. Script: James T. O'Donohue. Photography:
Barney McGill, John Marta, John Smith. Titles: M.S.
Boylan.
Cast: Victor McLaglen (Captain Flagg), Edmund
Lowe (Sergeant Quirk), Dolores Del Rio (Charmaine),
William V. Mong (Cognac Pete), Phyllis Haver (Hilda of
China), Elena Juarado (Carmen), Leslie Fenton (Lieu-
tenant Moore), August Tollaire (French Mayor), Barry
Norton (Private Lewisohn), Sammy Cohen (Private Lipin-
ski), Ted McNamara (Private Kiper), Mathilde Comont
(Camille, the cook), Pat Rooney (Mulcahy).

6. RESURRECTION (United Artists, 1927)
Production: Producer/Director: Edwin Carewe.
Script: Finis Fox, Edwin Carewe. Photography: Robert
Kurrle. Titles: Tom Miranda.
Cast: Rod La Rocque (Prince Dimitri Nekhludof),
Dolores Del Rio (Katusha Maslova), Marc MacDermott
(Major Schoenboch), Lucy Beaumont (Aunt Sophya), Vera
Lewis (Aunt Marya), Clarissa Selwynne (Princess Olga
Ivanovitch Nekhludof), Eve Southern (Princess Sonia
Korchagin).

7. LOVES OF CARMEN (Fox Film Corporation, 1927)
Production: Producer: William Fox. Director:
Raoul Walsh. Script: Gertrude Orr. Photography: Lucien
Andriot, John Marta. Titles: Katherine Hilliker, H.H.
Caldwell.
Cast: Dolores Del Rio (Carmen), Victor McLaglen
(Escamillo), Don Alvarado (Jose), Nancy Nash (Michaela),
Rafael Valverda (Miguel), Mathilde Comont (Emilia), Jack
Baston (Morales), Carmen Costello (Teresa), Fred Kohler
(Gypsy chief).

8. THE GATEWAY OF THE MOON (Fox Film Corporation, 1928)
Production: Producer: William Fox. Director: John
Griffith Wray. Script: Bradley King. Titles: Katherine
Hilliker, H.H. Caldwell. Photography: Chester Lyons.
Cast: Dolores Del Rio (Chela Toni), Walter Pidgeon
(Arthur Wyatt), Anders Randolf (George Gillespie), Ted
McNamara (Henry Hooker), Adolph Millar (Rudolf Gottman),
Leslie Fenton (Jim Mortlake), Noble Johnson (Soriano),
Virginia La Fonde (Indian child).

9. RAMONA (United Artists, 1928)
    Production: Director: Edwin Carewe. Scenario/
Titles: Finis Fox. Photography: Robert B. Kurrle, Al
M. Greene. Theme Song: Mabel Wayne - L. Wolfe Gilbert.
    Cast: Dolores Del Rio (Ramona), Warner Baxter
(Alessandro), Roland Drew (Felipe), Vera Lewis (Senora
Moreno), Michael Visaroff (Juan Canito), John T. Prince
(Father Salvierderra), Mathilde Comont (Marda), Carlos
Amor (sheepherder), Jess Cavin (bandit leader), Jean
(himself, a dog), Rita Carewe (baby).

10. NO OTHER WOMAN (Fox Film Corporation, 1928)
    Production: Producer: William Fox. Director: Lou
Tellegen. Scenario: Jesse Burns, Bernard Vorhaus.
Titles: Katherine Hilliker, H.H. Caldwell. Photography:
Ernest Palmer, Paul Ivano.
    Cast: Dolores Del Rio (Carmelita Desano), Don
Alvarado (Maurice), Ben Bard (Albert), Paulette Duval
(Mafalda), Rosita Marstini (Carmelita's aunt), Andre
Lanoy (Grand Duke Sergey).

11. THE RED DANCE (Fox Film Corporation, 1928)
    Production: Producer: William Fox. Director: Raoul
Walsh. Scenario: James A. Creelman. Titles: M.S. Boylan.
Photography: Charles Clarke, John Marta. Song: "Someday,
Somewhere, We'll Meet Again" (Lew Pollack - Erno Rapee).
    Cast: Charles Farrell (The Grand Duke Eugen),
Dolores Del Rio (Tasia), Ivan Linow (Ivan Petroff), Boris
Charsky (an agitator), Dorothy Revier (Princess Varvara),
Andres De Segurola (General Tanaroff), Demetrius Alexis
(Rasputin).

12. REVENGE (United Artists, 1928)
    Production: Producer/Director: Edwin Carewe.
Scenario/Titles: Finis Fox. Photography: Robert Kurrle,
Al M. Greene.
    Cast: Dolores Del Rio (Rascha), James Marcus (Costa),
Sophia Ortiga (Binka), LeRoy Mason (Jorga), Rita Carewe
(Tina), Jose Crespo (Stefan), Sam Appel (Jancu), Marta
Golden (Leana), Jess Cavin (Lieutenant De Jorga).

13. THE TRAIL OF '98 (Metro-Goldwyn-Mayer, 1929)
    Production: Director: Clarence Brown. Scenario:
Benjamin Glazer, Waldemar Young. Titles: Joe Farnham.
Photography: John Seitz. Art Directors: Cedric Gibbons,
Merrill Pye. Song: "I Found Gold When I Found You"
(Hazel Mooney - Evelyn Lyn-William Axt).

Cast: Dolores Del Rio (Berna), Ralph Forbes (Larry),
Karl Dane (Lars Petersen), Harry Carey (Jack Locasto),
Tully Marshall (Salvation Jim), George Cooper (Samuel
Foote, The Worm), Russell Simpson (Old Swede), Emily
Fitzroy (Mrs. Bulkey), Tenen Holtz (Mr. Bulkey), Cesare
Gravina (Berna's grandfather), E. Alyn Warren (engineer),
John Down (mother's boy), Ray Gallagher, Doris Lloyd.

14. EVANGELINE (United Artists, 1929)
      Production: Producer/Director: Edwin Carewe.
Scenario/Titles: Finis Fox. Photography: Robert B.
Kurrle, Al M. Greene.
      Cast: Dolores Del Rio (Evangeline), Roland Drew
(Gabriel), Alec B. Francis (Father Felician), Donald
Reed (Baptiste), Paul McAllister (Benedict Bellefon-
taine), James Marcus (Basil), George Marion, Sr. (René
La Blanc), Bobby Mack (Michael), Lou Payne (Governor-
General), Lee Shumway (Colonel Winslow).

15. THE BAD ONE (United Artists, 1930)
      Production: Producer: Joseph M. Schenck. Director:
George Fitzmaurice. Script: Carey Wilson, Howard Emmett
Rogers. Photography: Karl Strauss.
      Cast: Dolores Del Rio (Lita), Edmund Lowe (Jerry
Flanagan), Don Alvarado (Spaniard), Blanche Frederici
(Madame Durand), Adrienne D'Ambricourt (Madame Pompier),
Ullrich Haupt (Pierre Ferrande), Mitchell Lewis (Borloff),
Ralph Lewis (Blochet), Charles McNaughton (Petey), Yola
D'Avril (Gida), John St. Polis (judge), Henry Kolker
(prosecuting attorney), George Fawcett (warden), Victor
Potel, Harry Stubbs, Tommy Dugan (sailors).

16. GIRL OF THE RIO (RKO Radio Pictures, 1932)
      Production: Director: Herbert Brenon. Screenplay:
Elizabeth Meehan based on Willard Mack's The Dove.
      Cast: Dolores Del Rio (Dolores), Leo Carrillo (Don
José Tostado), Norman Foster (Johnny Powell), Lucille
Gleason (The Matron), Ralph Ince (O'Grady), Edna Murphy
(Madge), Stanley Fields (Mike), Frank Campeau (Bill),
Roberta Gale (Mabelle).

17. BIRD OF PARADISE (RKO Radio Pictures, 1932)
      Production: Producer: David O. Selznick. Director:
King Vidor. Screenplay: Wells Root, Leonard Praskins,
and Wanda Tuchock. Photography: Clyde De Vinna. Score:
Max Steiner. Choreography: Busby Berkeley.

Cast: Dolores Del Rio (Luana), Joel McCrea (Johnny Baker), John Halliday (Mac), Lon Chaney, Jr. (Thornton), Richard Gallagher (Chester), Bert Roach (Hector), Pului (The King), Agostino Borgato (Medicine Man), Sophie Ortego (Old Native Woman).

18. FLYING DOWN TO RIO (RKO Radio Pictures, 1933)
Production: Producer: Louis Brock. Director: Thorton Freeland. Songs: Vincent Youmans-Edward Eliscu-Gus Kahn. Screenplay: Cyril Hume, H.W. Hanemann, Erwin Gelsey. Dance Director: Dave Gould. Cameraman: J. Roy Hunt.
Cast: Dolores Del Rio (Belinha de Rezende), Gene Raymond (Roger Bond), Raul Roulien (Julio Rubeiro), Ginger Rogers (Honey Hale), Fred Astaire (Fred Ayres), Franklin Pangborn (Mr. Hammerstein), Eric Blore (Assistant Hotel Manager).

19. WONDER BAR (Warner Bros., 1934)
Production: Director: Lloyd Bacon. Screenplay: Earl Baldwin. Songs: Harry Warren-Al Dubin. Choreography: Busby Berkeley.
Cast: Al Jolson (Al Wonder), Kay Francis (Liane Renaud), Dolores Del Rio (Inez), Ricardo Cortez (Harry), Dick Powell (Tommy), Hal LeRoy (Hal LeRoy), Guy Kibbee (Mr. Simpson), Ruth Donnelly (Mrs. Simpson), Hugh Herbert (Mr. Pratt), Louise Fazenda (Mrs. Pratt), Fifi d'Orsay (Mitzi), Merna Kennedy (Claire), Henry Kolker (Mr. Renaud), Henry O'Neill (Richard), Robert Barrat (Captain von Ferring).

20. MADAME DU BARRY (Warner Bros., 1934)
Production: Director: William Dieterle. Screenplay: Edward Chorodov. Photography: Sol Polito. Art Director: Jack Okey.
Cast: Dolores Del Rio (Du Barry), Reginald Owen (Louis XV), Victor Jory (d'Alguillon), Osgood Perkins (Richelieu), Verree Teasdale (Duchess de Grammont), Ferdinand Gottschalk (Lebel), Dorothy Tree (Adelaide), Anita Louise (Marie Antoinette), Maynard Holmes (The Dauphin), Henry O'Neill (Duc de Choiseul), Hobart Cavanaugh (Professor de la Vauguyon), Helen Lowell (Countess de Berne), Joan Wheeler (Florette), Halliwell Hobbes (English Ambassador), Nella Walker (Mme. Noailics), Virginia Sale (Sophie), Arthur Treacher (Master of the Bedroom), Jesse Scott (Zamore), Camille Rovelie (Victoire).

21. IN CALIENTE (Warner Bros., 1935)
     Production: Director: Lloyd Bacon. Screenplay:
Jerry Wald and Julius Epstein. Photography: Sol Polito
and George Barnes. Choreography: Busby Berkeley.
     Cast: Dolores Del Rio (Rita Gomez), Pat O'Brien
(Larry MacArthur), Leo Carrillo (Jose Gomez), Edward
Everett Horton (Harold Brandon), Glenda Farrell (Clara),
The DeMarcos (Dance Team), The Canova Family (Musical
Quartet), Phil Regan (Singer), Dorothy Dare (The Girl),
Winifred Shaw (Singer), Luis Alberni (Magistrate), George
Humbert (Photographer).

22. I LIVE FOR LOVE (Warner Bros., 1935)
     Production: Produced: Bryan Foy. Directed: Busby
Berkeley. Screenplay: Jerry Wald, Julius J. Epstein,
and Robert Andrews. Photography: George Barnes. Songs:
Allie Wrubel-Mort Dixon.
     Cast: Dolores Del Rio (Donna Alvarez), Everett
Marshall (Roger Kerry), Guy Kibbee (George Henderson),
Allen Jenkins (Jim McNamara), Berton Churchill (Howard
Fabian), Don Alvarado (Rico Cesaro), Hobart Cavanaugh
(Howard Fabian).

23. THE WIDOW FROM MONTE CARLO (Warner Bros., 1936)
     Production: Directed: Arthur G. Collins. Screen-
play: F. Hugh Herbert, Charles Belden, and George Bricker.
Photography: Warren Lynch.
     Cast: Warren William (Chepstow), Dolores Del Rio
(Inez), Louise Fazenda (Mrs. Torrent), Colin Clive (Eric),
Herbert Mundin (Mr. Torrent), Olin Howland (Eaves), Warren
Hymer (Dopey), Ely Melyon (Lady Maynard), E.E. Clive
(Lord Holloway), Mary Forbes (Lady Holloway), Viva Tatter-
sall (Joan).

24. ACCUSED (United Artists-Criterion, Britain, 1936)
     Production: Producers: Marcel Hellman and Douglas
Fairbanks Jr. Director: Thornton Freeland. Screenplay:
Zoe Atkins, George Barraud and Harold French.
     Cast: Douglas Fairbanks Jr. (Tony Seymour), Dolores
Del Rio (Gaby Seymour), Florence Desmond (Yvette Delange),
Basil Sydney (Eugene Roget), John Roberts (Justice), Cecil
Humphries (Prosecuting counsel), Esme Percy (Morel),
Edward Rigby (Alphonse), George Moor Marriot (The Con-
cierge), Cyril Raymond (Gay Henry), Googie Withers (Ninette),
Roland Culver (Henry Capelle).

25. THE DEVIL'S PLAYGROUND (Columbia, 1937)
     Production: Director: Erle C. Kenton. Screenplay:
Liam O'Flaherty, Jerome Chorodov, Dalton Trumbo. Photo-
graphy: Lucien Ballard.
     Cast: Richard Dix (Jack Dorgan), Dolores Del Rio
(Carmen), Chester Morris (Robert Mason), George McKay
(Red Anderson), John Gallaudet (Jones), Pierre Watkins
(Submarine Commander), Ward Bond (Sidecar Wilson), Don
Rowan (Reilly), Francis McDonald (Romano), Stanley Andrews
(Salvage Boat Commander).

26. LANCER SPY (Twentieth-Century-Fox, 1937)
     Production: Producer: Samuel G. Engel. Director:
Irving Pichel. Screenplay: Philip Dunne. Photography:
Barney McGill.
     Cast: Dolores Del Rio (Fraulein Dolores Daria),
George Sanders (Lieutenant Michael Bruce), Peter Lorre
(Major Sigfried Gruning), Virginia Field (Joan Bruce),
Sig Rumann (Lieut. Col. Gottfried Hollen), Joseph Schild-
Kraut (Prince Ferdi zu Schwarzwald), Maurice Moscovich
(General Von Meinhardi), Lionel Atwill (Colonel Fenwick),
Luther Adler (Schratt), Fritz Feld (Fritz Mueller), Holmes
Herbert (Dr. Aldrich), Lester Matthews (Captain Neville),
Carlos de Valdez (Von Klingen), Gregory Gaye (Captain
Freymann), Joan Carol (Elizabeth Bruce), Kenneth Hunter
(Commandant), Frank Reicher (Admiral), Claude King (Cap-
tain), Leonard Mudie (Statesman).

27. INTERNATIONAL SETTLEMENT (Twentieth-Century-Fox, 1938)
     Production: Producer: Sol M. Wurtzel. Director:
Eugene Ford. Screenplay: Lou Breslow, John Patrick.
Songs: Sidney Clare-Harry Akst. Photography: Lucien
Andriot.
     Cast: Dolores Del Rio (Lenore Dixon), George Sanders
(Del Forbes), June Lang (Joyce Parker), Dick Baldwin
(Wally Burton), Ruth Terry (Specialty), John Carradine
(Murdock), Keye Luke (Dr. Wong), Harold Huber (Joseph
Lang), Leon Ames (Monte Silvers), Pedro de Cordoba
(Maurice Zabello).

28. THE MAN FROM DAKOTA (Metro-Goldwyn-Mayer, 1940)
     Production: Producer: Edward Chorodov. Director:
Leslie Fenton. Screenplay: Laurence Stallings. Photo-
graphy: Ray June.
     Cast: Wallace Beery (Sergeant Barstow), John Howard
(Oliver Clark), Dolores Del Rio (Jenny), Donald Meek
(Vestry), Robert Barrat (Parson Summers), Addison Richards

(Provost Marshal), Frederick Burton (Cambellite), William
Haade (Union soldier), John Wray (Mr. Carpenter).

29. JOURNEY INTO FEAR (RKO, 1942)
     Production: Screenplay: Joseph Cotton. Photo-
graphy: Karl Strauss. Director: Norman Foster and
Orson Welles.
     Cast: Joseph Cotton (Howard Graham), Dolores Del
Rio (Josette Martel), Ruth Warrick (Stephanie Graham),
Orson Welles (Colonel Haki), Agnes Moorehead (Mrs. Mat-
thews), Jack Durant (Gogo), Everett Sloane (Kopelkie),
Edgar Barrier (Kuvetli), Jack Moss (Banat), Stefan
Schnabel (Purser), Hans Conried (Magician), Richard
Bennett (Ship's Captain), Robert Meltzer (Steward).

30. FLOR SILVESTRE (Agustin-Fink-Films Mundiales, Mexico,
     1943).
     Production: Director: Emilio Fernández. Story:
Fernández and Mauricio Magdaleno. Based on the novel
Sucedió Ayer by Fernando Robles. Photography: Gabriel
Figueroa. Music: Francisco Domínguez.
     Cast: Dolores Del Rio (Esperanza), Pedro Armen-
dáriz (José Luis Castro), Emilio Fernandez (Rogellio
Torres), Miguel Angel Ferriz (Don Francisco Castro),
Chiocto (Reynaldo), Mimi Derba (Dona Clara), Edouardo
Arozomona (Melchor).

31. MARIA CANDELARIA (Films Mundiales, 1943).
     Production: Director: Emilio Fernández. Screen-
play: Fernández and Mauricio Magdeleno. Photography:
Gabriel Figueroa. Music: Francisco Domínguez.
     Cast: Dolores Del Rio (María Candelaria), Lorenzo
Rafael (Pedro Armendáriz), Lupe (Margarita Cortes), Alberto
Galán (El Pintor), Beatríz Ramos (Reporter), Manuel Inclan
(Don Damián), Rafael Icardo (Señor Cura), Julio Ahuet
(José Alfonso), Arturo Soto Rangel (Doctor).

32. BUGAMBILIA (Films Mundiales, 1944)
     Production: Director: Emilio Fernández. Screenplay:
Fernández and Mauricio Magdeleno. Photography: Gabriel
Figueroa. Music: Raúl Lavista.
     Cast: Dolores Del Rio (Amalia de los Robles), Pedro
Armendáriz (Ricardo Rojas), Julio Villarreal (don Fernando),
Alberto Galán (Luis Felipe), Stella Inda (Zarca), Paco
Fuentes (don Enrique, juez), Arturo Soto Rangel (cura),
Elba Alvarez (Mercedes), Concha Sanz (nana Nicanora),
Maruja Grifell (Matilde, chismosa).

33. LAS ABANDONADAS (Films Mundiales, 1944)
Production: Director: Emilio Fernández. Screen-
play Fernández and Mauricio Magdaleno. Photography:
Gabriel Figueroa. Music: Manuel Esperón.
Cast: Dolores Del Rio, Pedro Armendáriz, Arturo,
Soto Rangel, Fanny Schiller, Maruja Grifell, Lupe Inclán.

34. LA SELVA DE FUEGO (Diana, 1945)
Production: Director: Fernando de Fuentes.
Screenplay: Antonio Mediz Bolio and Paulino Masip.
Photography: Agustín Martínez Solares.
Cast: Arturo de Córdova, Dolores Del Rio,
Miguel Inclán, Felipe Montoya, Daniel Herrera, José
Laboriel.

35. LA OTRA (Mercurio, 1946)
Production: Director: Roberto Gavaldón. Screen-
play: Galvaldón and José Revueltas. Photography:
Alex Phillips. Music: Manuel Esperón.
Cast: Dolores Del Rio, Agustín Irusta, Víctor
Junco, José Baviera, Manuel Dondé, Conchita Carracedo,
Carlos Villarías, Rafael Icardo.

36. THE FUGITIVE (RKO, 1947)
Production: Producer: John Ford and Merian C.
Cooper. Screenplay: Dudley Nichols. Director: John
Ford. Photography: Gabriel Figueroa.
Cast: Henry Fonda (A Fugitive), Dolores Del Rio
(an Indian Woman), Pedro Armendariz (Lieutenant of
Police), J. Carrol Naish (Police Informer), Leo Carrillo
(Chief of Police), Ward Bond (El Gringo), Robert Arm-
strong (Sergeant of Police), John Qualen (A Refugee
Doctor), Fortunio Bonanova (The Governor's Cousin),
Cris-Pin Martin (Organ-Grinder), Miguel Inclan (A Hostage),
Fernando Fernandez (A Singer).

37. HISTORIA DE UNA MALA MUJER (Argentine Sono, 1948)
Production: Director: Luis Saslavsky. Adapted
by Pedro Miguel Obligado from Oscar Wilde's Lady
Windermere's Fan. Photography: Alberto Etchebehere.
Music: Victor Slister.
Cast: Dolores Del Rio, María Duval, Francisco de
Paula, Alberto Closas, Fernando Lamas, Amalia Sánchez
Ariño.

38. LA MALQUERIDA (Cabrera, 1949)
Production: Director: Emilio Fernández. Screenplay: Fernández and Mauricio Magdaleno. Photography:

Gabriel Figueroa. Music: Antonio Díaz Conde.
     Cast: Dolores Del Rio, Pedro Armendáriz, Columba
Domínguez, Roberto Cañedo, Julio Villarreal, Mimí Derba.

39. LA CASA CHICA (Filmex, 1949)
     Production: Director: Roberto Gavaldón. Screen-
play: Gavaldón and José Revueltas. Photography: Alex
Phillips. Music: Antonio Díaz Conde.
     Cast: Dolores Del Rio, Roberto Cañedo, Miroslava,
Domingo Soler, María Douglas, José Elías Moreno, Arturo
Soto Rangel.

40. DESEADA (Sanson, 1950)
     Production: Director: Roberto Gavaldón. Screen-
play: José Revueltas and Antonio Mediez Bolio.
Photography: Alex Phillips. Music: Eduardo Hernández
Moncada.
     Cast: Dolores Del Rio, Jorge Mistral, Anabelle
Gutiérrez, Arturo Soto Rangel.

41. DOÑA PERFECTA (Cabrera Films, 1950)
     Production: Director: Alejandro Galindo. Screen-
play: Galindo, based on a novel by Benito Pérez Galdos
Photography: José Ortiz Ramos. Music: Gustavo César
Garrión.
     Cast: Dolores Del Rio, Carlos Navarro, Julio
Villarreal, Esther Fernández.

42. REPORTAJE (Periodístas Cinematográficos Mexicanos
A.A. y Asociación Nacional de Actores, 1953)
     Production: Director: Emilio Fernández. Screen-
play: Fernández and Mauricio Magdaleno. Photography:
Alex Phillips. Music: Antonio Díaz Conde.
     Cast: Dolores Del Rio, Arturo de Córdova, Jorge
Negrete, María Felix, Libertad Lamarque, Pedro Armend-
áriz, María Elena Marqués, Roberto Cañedo, Pedro Infante,
Sarita Montiel, Víctor Parra, Julio Villarreal, Antonio
Espino "Clavillazo".

43. EL NIÑO Y LA NIEBLA (Grovas, 1953)
     Production: Director: Roberto Gavaldón. Screen-
play: Edmundo Báez and Gavaldón based on a work by
Rodolfo Usigli. Photography: Gabriel Figueroa.
Music: Raul Lavista.
     Cast: Dolores Del Rio, Pedro López Lagar, Eduardo
Noriega, Alejandro Ciangherotti hijo, Miguel Angel
Ferriz, Carlos Riquelme.

44. SEÑORA AMA (Union Films, Spain, 1954)
      Production: Director: Julio Bracho. Screenplay:
Julio Bracho. Photography: Ted Pahle. Music:
Salvador Ruiz de Luna.
      Cast: Dolores Del Rio, José Suárez, Manuel
Monroy.

45. A DONDE VAN NUESTROS HIJOS (Filmex, 1956)
      Production: Director and Screenplay: Benito
Alazraki. Photography: Agustín Martínez Solares.
      Cast: Dolores Del Rio, Tito Junco, Ana Bertha
Lupe, Martha Mijares, León Michel, Carlos Fernández,
Rogelio Jiménez Pons, Carlos Rivas, Carlos Riquelme,
Luis Aragón, Héctor Godoy.

46. LA CUCARACHA (Películas Rodríguez, 1958)
      Production: Director: Ismael Rodríguez. Screen-
play: José Luis Celis, Ricardo Garibay, and Rodríguez
      Cast: María Félix, Dolores Del Rio, Emilio
Fernández, Ignacio López Tarso, Tony Aguilar, Lupe
Carriles, Pedro Armendáriz, Guillermina Jiménez,
Miguel Manzano, Cuco Sánchez, Alicia del Lago.

47. EL PECADO DE UNA MADRE (Brooks, 1960)
      Production: Director: Alfonso Corona Blake.
Screenplay: Julio Alejandro de Castro. Photography:
Jack Draper.
      Cast: Libertad Lamarque, Dolores Del Rio, Pedro
Geraldo, Tete Velázquez, Luis Beristáin, Eduardo Alcaraz,
Julián de Meriche, Antonio Raxell, Enrique Rambal.

48. FLAMING STAR (Twentieth-Century-Fox, 1960)
      Production: Producer: David Weisbart. Director:
Don Siegel. Screenplay: Clair Huffaker and Nunnally
Johnson. Photography: Charles G. Clarke. Music:
Cyril J. Mockridge.
      Cast: Elvis Presley (Pacer Burton), Steve Forrest
(Clint Burton), John McIntire (Pa Burton), Dolores Del
Rio (Neddy Burton), Barbara Eden (Roslyn Pierce),
Rudolph Acosta (Buffalo Horn), Karl Swenson (Dred Pierce),
Ford Rainey (Doc Phillips), Richard Jaeckel (Angus Pierce),
Anne Benton (Dorothy Howard), Douglas Dick (Will Howard),
L. Q. Jones (Tom Howard), Perry Lopez (Two Moons), Tom
Reese (Jute), Monte Burkhart (Ben Ford), Ted Jacques
(Hornsby), Marian Goldina (Ph Sha Knay), Rodd Redwing
(Indian Brave).

49. CHEYENNE AUTUMN (Warner Bros., 1964)
     Production: Producer:John Ford and Bernard Smith.
Director: John Ford. Screenplay: James R. Webb.
     Cast: Richard Widmark (Capt. Thomas Archer),
Carroll Baker (Deborah Wright), Karl Malden (Captain
Wessels), Sal Mineo (Red Shirt), Dolores Del Rio
(Spanish Woman), Ricardo Montalban (Little Wolf),
Gilbert Roland (Dull Knife), Arthur Kennedy (Doc Holliday),
James Stewart (Wyatt Earp), Edward G. Robinson (Carl
Schurz), Patrick Wayne (Second Lieutenant Scott),
Elizabeth Allen (Miss Plantagenet), John Carradine (Jeff
Blair), Victor Jory (Tall Tree), Mike Mazurki (Senior
First Sergeant), George O'Brien (Major Braden), Sean
McClory (Dr. O'Carberry), Judson Pratt (Mayor Dog
Kelly), Carmen D'Antonio (Pawnee Woman), Ken Curtis
(Joe).

50. LA DAMA DEL ALBA (Spain, 1966)
     Production: Director: Rovira Beleta.
     Cast: Dolores Del Rio, Elena Samarina, Juliette
Villars, Daniel Martin.

51. CASA DE MUJERES (Amador, 1966)
     Production: Director: Julián Soler, Screenplay:
Alfredo Varela. Photography: José Ortiz Ramos.
Music: Manuel Esperón.
     Cast: Dolores Del Rio, Elsa Aguirre, Rosa María
Vázquez, Martha Romero, Elsa Cárdenas, María Duval.

52. MORE THAN A MIRACLE (Metro-Goldwyn-Mayer, 1967)
     Production: Producer: Carlo Ponti. Director:
Francesco Rosi. Screenplay: Tonino Guerra, Raffaele
La Capria, Giuseppe Patroni Griffi, Francesco Rosi.
Title Song: Larry Kusik, Eddie Snyder, Piero Piccioni.
     Cast: Sophia Loren (Isabella), Omar Sharif
(Prince Ramon), Dolores Del Rio (Princess Mother),
Georges Wilson (Monzu), Leslie French (Brother Joseph),
Carlo Pisacane (1st witch), Marina Malfatti (devout
princess), Anna Nogara (impatient princess), Rita
Forzano (greedy princess), Rosemary Martin (vain prin-
cess), Carlotta Barilli (superstitious princess), Fleur
Mombelli (haughty princess), Anna Liotti (infant prin-
cess), Cris Huerta (Spanish groom), Pietro Carloni
(village priest), Giovanni Tarallo (elderly monk),
Renato Pinciroli (prince's chamberlain), Giacomo Furia
(prior), Gladys Dawson, Kathleen St. John, Beatrice
Greack (head witches), Pasquale Di Napoli, Francesco
Coppola, Salvatore Ruvo, Vincenzo Danaro, Luciano Di Mauro,

Luigi Criscuolo, Francesco Lo Como (street urchins),
Valentino Macchi.

53. RIO BLANCO (Galindo Brothers, 1967)
     Production: Roberto Gavaldón, Screenplay: Roberto
Gavaldón and Tito Davidson.
     Cast: Silvia Pinal, Ignacio Lopez Tarso, David
Reynoso.

TELEVISION PERFORMANCES

1. SCHLITZ PLAYHOUSE (CBS) June 7, 1957.
         Episode: An Old Spanish Custom.
         Synopsis: A tempermental movie star believes
    she can issue orders to everyone - even people
    she's just met. When her new neighbor, a horse
    trainer, comes over to use her telephone, she
    begins to issue him orders too. But he refuses
    to obey.
         Cast: Dolores Del Rio (Delores Delgado),
    Cesar Romero (Luis Mendoza), Murray Hamilton
    (Arnold), Leon Askin (Senor Valdez), Celia Lovsky
    (Señora Valdez), Belle Mitchell (Dona Ana).

2. U. S. STEEL HOUR (CBS) April 23, 1958.
         Episode: The Public Prosecutor.
         Synopsis: In eighteenth century Paris during
    the reign of terror, Theresa Tallien, wife of the
    head of the governmnet, devises a plan to eliminate
    the powerful and heartless public prosecutor
    Fouquier-Tinville, who is using his position to
    further his own ends. Mme. Tallien intends to trap
    him through his own cunning devices.
         Writer: Theodore Apstein.
         Cast: Walter Slezak (Fouquier-Tinville), Frank
    Conroy (Montaine), Jerome Kilty (Grebauval),
    Alexander Clark (Heron), Ben Hayes (Fabricius).

3.   I SPY (NBC) February 23, 1966.
         Episode: Return to Glory
         Synopsis: In Mexico City, Robinson and Scott
    get a delicate assignment: The State Department
    wants them to contact deposed dictator, Rafael Ortiz
    to find out what assistance Ortiz will need for a
    return to power.
         A meeting with Ortiz is arranged, but he fails
    to appear. His wife Cerita and a mercenary insist
    that it is too dangerous for the general to be seen
    in public. This seems like a reasonable explanation,
    but attempts to see Ortiz in private are also un-
    successful.
         Producers/Writers: Morton Fine and David Friedkin.
         Cast: Robert Culp (Robinson), Bill Cosby (Scott),
    Dolores Del Rio (Cerita), Victor Jory (Rafael Ortiz),
    Mark Dana (Martin), Antoinette Bower (Shelby),
    Roberto Iglesias (Cordoba).

4. BRANDED (NBC) March 20, 1966.
   Episode: The Ghost of Murrieta
   Synopsis: Los Angeles teen-ager Juan Molinera
hopes to emulate the infamous bandit Murrieta by
stealing the $50,000 in gold entrusted to McCord.
   Cast: Chuck Connors (McCord), Dolores Del Rio
(Antonia Molinera), Jose De Vega (Juan Molinera),
Linda Dangcil (Rosita), Rafael Campos (Luis), Ben
Welden (Vega), Robert Tafur (Ramírez), George de
Anda (Pablo), George Petrie (Hartley).

5. MARCUS WELBY, M.D. (ABC) January 27, 1970.
   Episode: The Legacy
   Synopsis: The story of two gravely ill women
facing the prospect of death. Carlotta Lopez taps
wellsprings of love and faith to make a poignant
decision about the time she has left. Anne Faris
minimizes her chances with an attitude steeped with
bitterness and spite.
   Cast: Robert Young (Welby), James Brolin (Kiley),
Elena Verdugo (Consuelo), Dolores Del Rio (Carlotta
Lopez), Janet Blair (Anne Faris), John Roper
(Ricardo), Inez Pedroza (Margarita).

NOTES

Chapter I.   THE LATIN IMAGE IN SILENT FILMS.

1.   See: Terry Ramsaye, A Million and One Nights: A History of the Motion Picture (New York, 1964).

2.   See: Blaine P. Lamb, "The Convenient Villain," Journal of the West (October, 1975), 75-81.

3.   See: George Roeder, "The Image of the Mexican," (Unpublished mss., University of Wisconsin, 1971).

4.   Moving Picture World, 22 (October, 1914).

5.   Ibid., 22 (September, 23, 1914).

6.   Ibid., 21 (July, 1914), 84.

7.   Kevin Brownlow, The Parade's Gone By (New York, 1968), 224.

8.   Raoul Walsh, Each Man In His Own Time (New York, 1974), 86.

9   Brownlow, The Parade's Gone By, 224

10.   Moving Picture World, 21 (July 18, 1914), 440.

11.   New York Times (henceforth NYT), May 10, 1914.

12.   Moving Picture World, 21 (July, 1914), 80.

13.   Ibid., 22 (October, 1914), 467.

14.   Ibid., 27 (March 18, 1916).

15.   Ibid., 28 (April 22, 1916), 84

16.   Ibid., 34 (December 22, 1917), 1796.

17.   Ibid., 32 (May 5, 1917), 789, 955.

18.   Ibid., 27 (March 25, 1916), 1983.

19.   Ibid., 22 (October 1, 1914), 467.

20.   Ibid., 27 (March 25, 1916), 1983.

21.   Ibid., 36 (May 20, 1918), 1546. See also: New York Evening Sun, May 20, 1918.

22. <u>Ibid</u>., 31 (March 17, 1925), 20.

23. <u>Ibid</u>., 40 (April 26, 1919), 532.

24. <u>NYT</u>, February 11, 1922, 15.

25. <u>Ibid</u>., May 1, 1923.

26. <u>Ibid</u>., September 19, 1926.

27. <u>Ibid</u>., December 28, 1924.

28. <u>Ibid</u>., October 16, 1927.

29. <u>NYT</u>, January 3, 1928.

30. <u>Ibid</u>., April 3, 1927.

Chapter II: DOLORES DEL RIO--THE EARLY YEARS

1.   "Dolores Del Rio Flouted Both Tradition and Advice
     To Leave Quiet Mexican Home and Achieve Stardom,"
     Del Rio File, Philadelphia Library Theater Collection,
     no date.

2.   José Gómez-Sicre, "Dolores Del Rio," <u>Américas</u>
     (November, 1967), 8-9.

3.   "Dolores Del Rio Flouted Both Tradition and Advice,"
     <u>op</u>. <u>cit</u>.

4.   <u>Ibid</u>.

5.   <u>Ibid</u>.

6.   "Success With a Cup of Tea," <u>Motion Picture Classic</u>
     (March, 1927), 48-49.

7.   De Witt Bodeen, "Dolores Del Rio," <u>Films In Review</u>
     (May, 1967), 266-267.

Chapter III:

1. Gómez-Sicre, "Dolores Del Rio," 8-9

2. The American Film Institute Catalog of Motion Pictures Produced in the United States: Feature Films, 1921-1930 (New York, 1971). Synopses of Del Rio's early films are adapted from this source.

3. Walsh, Each Man In His Own Time, 186-187

4. Ibid., 193-194.

5. Ibid., 187.

6. Ibid., 186-187

7. Motion Picture (June, 1930), 59.

8. October 8, 1927, 381

9. Walsh, Each Man In His Own Time, 200

10. NYT, February 19, 1928, VII, 6.

11. Ibid., June 9, 1928.

12. Ibid. December 6,7,8,9, 1928; April 4, 1929.

13. Motion Picture Classic, August, 1928, 23, 72.

14. Motion Picture (June, 1930), 59, 90.

15. Ibid., 90.

Chapter IV: THE CHALLENGE OF SOUND

1. NYT, August 19, 1928.

2. Ibid., July 24, 1930.

3. Photoplay, April, 1934.

4. NYT, July 31, 1930; August 7, 1930.

5. Photoplay, August, 1931.

6. <u>NYT</u>, April 20, 1932.

7. Tony Thomas and Jim Terry, <u>The Busby Berkeley Book</u>, (Greenwich, Conn., 1973), 45.

8. Arlene Croce, <u>The Fred Astaire and Ginger Rogers Book</u> (New York, 1972), 23-29.

9. Tony Thomas and Jim Terry, <u>The Busby Berkeley Book</u>, 74-75.

10. <u>NYT</u>, December 17, 1936.

11. <u>Ibid</u>, February 15, 1937.

12. <u>Ibid</u>, February 12, 1938.

13. <u>Ibid</u>.

14. <u>Ibid</u>., February 6, 1938.

15. <u>Ibid</u>., March 17, 1940.

Chapter V: DEL RIO IN MEXICO.

1. Lincoln Hayes, "Mexican Movies Grow Up," <u>Theatre Arts</u> (November, 1951), 47, 86-87; Walker Lowry, "Movies With A Latin Accent, "<u>New York Times Magazine</u> (November 14, 1948).

2. See: Luis Reyes De La Maza, <u>El Cine Sónoro en México</u> (Mexico City, 1973).

3. José Gómez-Sicre, "Depth Of Focus," <u>Américas</u> (May, 1950).

4. Since many of Del Rio's Mexican films are not available in the United States many plot synopses are adapted from Emilio García Riera's monumental <u>Historia documental del cine Mexicano</u> (Mexico City). This several volume work documents the history of the Mexican cinema from its beginnings to modern times.

5. <u>NYT</u>, January 16, 1945, 17.

6. See <u>Ibid</u>., September 12, 1944, 23.

7.   <u>Ibid</u>., November 2, 1961, 42.

Chapter VI: RETURN TO HOLLYWOOD

1.   <u>The</u> <u>New</u> <u>York</u> <u>Times</u> <u>Magazine</u>, March 23, 1947, 17.

2.   Frederick C. Turner, <u>The</u> <u>Dynamic</u> <u>of</u> <u>Mexican</u> <u>National</u>-
     <u>ism</u> (Chapel Hill, 1968), 139. See also: Michael
     Wilmington, "Ford's <u>The</u> <u>Fugitive</u>," <u>The</u> <u>Velvet</u> <u>Light</u>
     <u>Trap</u> (Madison, Wisconsin), No. 5.

3.   <u>NYT</u>, March 3, 1954.

4.   <u>Ibid</u>., March 6, 1954.

5.   <u>Ibid</u>., April 20, 1958

6.   Bodeen, "Dolores Del Rio.", 276.

7.   <u>Films</u> <u>And</u> <u>Filming</u>, March, 1961, 29.

8.   Dee Brown, <u>Bury</u> <u>My</u> <u>Heart</u> <u>At</u> <u>Wounded</u> <u>Knee</u>, (New York,1971)
     Ch. 14.

9.   <u>NYT</u>, November 2, 1967.

10. <u>Architectural</u> <u>Digest</u>, (November/December, 1976), 123.

Chapter VII: AT PRESENT

1.   <u>Excelsior</u>, (Mexico City), April 23, 1976.

BIBLIOGRAPHY

I. <u>FILMS</u>

I would like to thank Susan Dalton and the
University of Wisconsin Center for Theater Research
for the opportunity to see all the RKO and Warner
Brothers films discussed in this text. The Theater
Collection of the Philadelphia Free Library and the
Annenberg Library of the University of Pennsylvania
provided reference materials, photographs, and
articles on Dolores Del Rio. The Library of Congress
graciously provided a print of <u>Cheyenne Autumn</u>.

II. <u>ARTICLES</u>

Albert, K. "Dolores vs. The Jinx," <u>Photoplay</u>
(August, 1931), 40-43.

Bean, Robin. "Flaming Star," <u>Films and Filming</u>
(March, 1961). 29.

Beery, R. "How Many Lives Has Dolores Del Rio?,"
<u>Photoplay</u> (October, 1933), 44-45.

Bodeen, De Witt. "Dolores Del Rio," <u>Films In
Review</u> (May, 1967), 266-283.

Braun, Eric. "Queen of Mexico," <u>Films and Filming</u>
(July, 1972), 34-38.

Gómez-Sicre, J. "Dolores Del Rio." <u>Américas</u>
November, 1967), 9-17.

Hayes, Lincoln. "Mexican Movies Grow Up," <u>Theatre
Arts</u> (November, 1951), 47, 86-87.

Hunt, J. L. "The Beauty Who Sits Alone," <u>Photoplay</u>
(December, 1934), 47-51.

Lieber, E. "What Price Stardom?" <u>Photoplay</u>
(September, 1932), 42-44.

Lowry, Walker. "Movies With a Latin Accent," <u>New
York Times Magazine</u> (November 14, 1948).

Potenze, Jaime. "Argentine Movies," <u>Américas</u>
(August, 1954).

Woll, Allen. "Hollywood's Good Neighbor Policy," *Journal of Popular Film* (Fall, 1974)

-----. "From Bandit to President: Latin Images in American Film, 1929-1939, "*Journal of Mexican-American History* (December, 1974)

III.   BOOKS

Brownlow, Kevin. *The Parade's Gone By*. New York, 1968.

Croce, Arlene. *The Fred Astaire and Ginger Rogers Book*. London, 1972.

Di Nubila, Domingo. *Historia del cine argentino*. Buenos Aires, 1959.

Fuente, María Isabel de la. *Indice bibliográfico del cine mexicano* (1930-1965). Mexico City, 1967.

García Riera, Emilio. *Historia documental del cine mexicano*. Mexico City, 1960.

Hijar, Alberto, ed. *Hacia un tercer cine*. Mexico City, 1972

Martínez Torres, Augusto and Perez Estremera, Manuel. *Nuevo cine latinoamericano*. Barcelona, 1973.

Maza, Luis Reyes De La. *El Cine Sónoro en México*. Mexico City, 1973.

Ramsaye, Terry. *A Million and One Nights*. New York, 1964.

Roeder, George. *The Image of the Mexican*. unpub. mss., University of Wisconsin, 1971.

Sennett, Ted. *Warner Brothers Presents*. New York, 1971.

Thomas, Tony and Terry, Jim. *The Busby Berkeley Book* New York, 1973.

Walsh, Raoul. *Each Man In His Own Time*. New York, 1974

Woll, Allen. *The Latin Image In American Film*,
  1894-1977. Los Angeles, 1977.

IV.   PERIODICALS AND MAGAZINES

Américas
Etude
Excelsior (Mexico City)
Filmfacts
Films In Review
Literary Digest
Movie Classic
Motion Picture
Motion Picture Classic
Motion Picture Herald
Moving Picture World
The Nation
New Republic
New York Evening Sun
New York Times
Newsweek
Photoplay
Politics
La Prensa (Buenos Aires)
Saturday Evening Post
Theatre Arts
Time
Vanity Fair
Variety
The Velvet Light Trap